The Chicago Landmark Project

With Short Plays by Brooke Berman, J. Nicole Brooks, Aaron Carter, Lonnie Carter, Brian Golden, Laura Jacqmin, Jamil Khoury, Rob Koon, Brett Neveu, Yolanda Nieves, Marisa Wegrzyn and The Red Orchid Youth Ensemble

Co-Coordinated by Brian Golden & Cassy Sanders

Produced by Theatre Seven of Chicago

THEATRE SEVEN OF CHICAGO

Copyright © 2011 by Theatre Seven of Chicago
All rights reserved

Published by Theatre Seven of Chicago
1341 W Fullerton Ave.
Suite 325
Chicago, IL 60614

Cover Design by Rebecca McCowan

First Edition: June 2011

CAUTION: Professionals and amateurs are hereby warned that plays represented in this book are subject to a royalty. They are fully protected by the copyright laws of the United States of America and of all countries covered by the international Copyright Union (included the Dominion of Canada and the rest of the British Commonwealth), the Berne Convention, the Pan-American Copyright Convention and the University Copyright Convention, as well as all rights, including professional and amateur stage rights, motion picture, recitation, lecturing, public reading, radio broadcasting, television, video or sound recording, all other forms of mechanical or electronic reproduction, such as CD-ROM, CD-I, DVD, information storage and retrieval systems and photocopying, and the rights of translation into foreign languages, are strictly reserved. Particular emphasis is laid upon the matter of readings, permission for which must be secured in writing. See individual plays for contact information.

ISBN-13: 978-1463573935
ISBN-10: 1463573936

Contents

Special Thanks	4
Theatre Seven of Chicago	5
About The Chicago Landmark Project	7
Foreword	8
State & Madison: The Chicago Grid	11
Lincoln & Webster: Oz Park	29
Garfield & State: Midway Liquors	47
Ohio & The Lake: Navy Pier	61
Division & California: Steel Flags	79
Logan & Milwaukee: Logan Square Farmers Market	91
63rd & Woodlawn: Robust Coffee Lounge	107
Lincoln & Eastwood: Laurie's Planet of Sound	129
Devon & Kedzie: Thillens Stadium	149
Honore & Milwaukee: Una Mae's Freak Boutique	163
63rd & Kedzie: Arab American Community Center	181
Belmont & Western: Riverview Amusement Park	195
Essay: *The Value of Local in a Global World*	219
A Final Thank You	221

Special Thanks

Greenhouse Theater Center
Jenn Kincaid
Maureen Strobel
Ralph Lopez
Una Mae's Freak Boutique
Carol Fox & Associates
Jenny Topolosky
Alex Garday
Derek Zasky
William Morris Endeavor Entertainment
Seth Glewen
The Gersh Agency
Logan Square Preservation
Lewis Coulson
Orion Couling
Tall Ship Windy
Chicago Dramatists
A Red Orchid Theatre
Neighborhood Writing Alliance
Silk Road Theatre Project
Malik Gillani
Rachael Hudak
Erin Moore
Carlos Flores
Books Plus Publications
Maddi Amill
Alderman Joe Moreno
Alderman Rey Colon
Robust Coffee Lounge
Steppenwolf Theatre Company
Andy Lutz
Jake Sapstein
Jessica Hutchinson
Laurie's Planet of Sound
Thillens Stadium
Southwest Youth Collective
Erica Daniels
Halcyon Theatre
Andrew Preston
Catharsis Productions
Vanessa Passini
Pat Fries
Maggie Fullilove-Nugent
The Saints
The Richard M. Driehaus Foundation
The Gaylord and Dorothy Donnelley Foundation
Chicago Community Trust
City Arts Assistance Program
JP Morgan Chase
Nancy Becker
Jip Jop
Liz Townsend
New Wave Coffee
David Keel
Open Source Theatre Project
Dani Bryant
Act One Studios
Paige Collins
Matt Farabee
Volen Iliev

Theatre Seven of Chicago Ensemble, June 2011

Company
Brian Golden, Margot Bordelon, Tracey Kaplan, Dan McArdle, Cassy Sanders, Brian Stojak, Justin Wardell, Marisa Wegrzyn, Brenda Winstead, George Zerante

Board of Directors
Barbara Agdern, Andrew Chao, Jill Davidson, Brian Golden, Paul Hybel, Rebecca Silverman, Carol White

Administrative Staff & Collaborators

Managing Artistic Director	Brian Golden
General Manager	Dan McArdle
Development Director	Rebecca Silverman
Director of Audience Services	Ben Brownson
Director of Audience Engagement	Taylor Fenderbosch
Community Manager	Jonathan Baude
Design Associate	Kate Rosendale
Development Associate	Kate Healy
Artistic Associate	Emily Grosland
Artistic Associate	Amanda Clifford
Artistic Associate	Alina Taber
Artistic Associate	Rebecca McCowan
Production Associate	Harriet Sogin

Company Members Emeritus
Robin Kacyn, Charlie Olson

Theatre Seven of Chicago produces new and original work that speaks directly to the diverse Chicago community with imagination and clarity. Since 2007, the company has produced thirteen standout offerings, including ten Chicago premieres. Theatre Seven's noted World Premieres include *Diversey Harbor* ("Hottest Ticket in Town" – Chicago Tribune), *Yes, This Really Happened To Me* (Critic's Choice – Chicago Reader), and *Cooperstown*, which earned the company nominations for one Jeff Award and two Black Theatre Alliance Awards. In both 2010 and 2011, Theatre Seven was named of one five finalists for the Emerging Theatre Award, presented by Broadway in Chicago and the League of Chicago Theatres. The company is funded with the generous support of the Chicago Community Trust, Richard M. Driehaus Foundation, Gaylord and Dorothy Donnelley Foundation, The Saints and the City Arts Assistance Program.

Production History

2007
Is Chicago: Two Stories, One City
Killing Women

2008
Boys & Girls
Yes, This Really Happened to Me
Election Day
The Sand Castle

2009
Diversey Harbor
Lies and Liars
Cooperstown

2010
Mimesophobia
Hunting and Gathering

2010-11
The Water Engine: An American Fable
The Chicago Landmark Project

The Chicago Landmark Project Production Team

Co-Coordinator & Dramaturg:	Brian Golden
Co-Coordinator & Dramaturg:	Cassy Sanders
Prod. Manager & Casting Coordinator:	Nick Ward
Production Stage Manager:	Taylor Fenderbosch
Production Stage Manager:	Jeri Frederickson
Set Designer:	Brandon Wardell
Supervising Light Designer:	Justin Wardell
Supervising Costume Designer:	Brenda Winstead
Sound Designer:	Joe Court
Props Designer:	Sarah Burnham
Props Designer:	Angela Campos
Light Designer:	Stephanie Bell
Costume Designer:	Julia Zayas-Melendez
Asst. Stage Manager:	Hannah Herbert
Asst. Stage Manager:	Sarah Hoeferlin
Technical Director:	Mike Smallwood
Fight Choreographer:	Vanessa Passini
Logan Square Composer:	Andy Lutz
AROT Production Manager:	Becky Blomgren
AROT Asst. Director:	Elise Lammers

Community Team

Ben Brownson
Taylor Fenderbosch
Brian Golden
Allyson Gonzalez
Sarah Grant
Kate Healy
Kim Morris
Cassy Sanders
Rebecca Silverman
Jessica Thigpen

Foreword

In early 2010, we conceived of the idea to commission multiple writers to tell Chicago stories as part of one theatrical production. The story of our journey in creating a piece of art deeply committed to community is also the story of a community of artists united around the central goal of *The Chicago Landmark Project*: to make a theatre piece that pays tribute to Chicago, past and present, by celebrating the diversity of its people and places and, in doing so, looks ahead to its future.

Our original intention, almost eighteen months ago, was to commission three Chicago playwrights to write one-act plays to run in repertory. As we began to conceptualize the project, we realized that no three plays could generate the comprehensive vision of Chicago we hoped to create, and our ambition doubled, with a new plan to include six short plays as one evening of theatre.

At this point, in June of 2010, we initiated conversations with a dozen playwrights whose work we admired, thinking that some might be busy with other commissions, a couple may be not interested in writing for the project, one or two may not be good fits, and that we'd end up with a team of about six.

To our surprise and delight, every playwright we approached about the project reacted with passion and enthusiasm at the opportunity to tell a Chicago story. We were blown away at the depth of insight each writer brought to our conversations about this city and the breadth of perspectives every one of them contributed to our vision of what the project could become.

Based on these conversations, with the support of the entire Theatre Seven of Chicago ensemble, we decided again to double the scope of the project to now include twelve Chicago stories, in the hopes of offering our audience an expansive, diverse and true vision of the city that would rival any in Chicago's theatre history.

To begin the creative process, we gave each of our playwrights two restrictions: every play in the project must deal with the question

How does location impact relationship? And in each case, the location in question must be an actual Chicago place, past or present. The final product of the work created by our writers under those two guidelines is *The Chicago Landmark Project,* a single production harnessing the talents of nearly 100 artists working together to put on stage the story of a city and its people.

We are indebted to our twelve playwrights, whose words so lovingly evoke the rhythms and emotions of our city, our twelve directors, who have been flexible, talented and consistently committed to the vision of the project, our thirty-five actors, who represent some of the best, most diverse talent, in the entire city, our tireless production team, led by Nick Ward, Taylor Fenderbosch, Jeri Frederickson and the entire design staff, who worked endlessly to realize the vision of all twelve plays while bringing the entire production together seamlessly and gracefully.

We must thank the nine members of our Community Team, who volunteered their time helping us achieve one of the most challenging aspects of the project – our goal to bring each play to the neighborhood of its setting for a Free Theatre Night.

We are incredibly grateful to the entire Theatre Seven ensemble for supporting our work, to our Board of Directors and to every donor whose contributions have been spent making this dream a reality, particularly those supporters whose sponsorship directly financed specific portions of this project; Harold & Carol Asher, Edith Taber & James Moore, Julia Lamber, Freddi Greenberg & Daniel Pinkert, Dan & Sheila Stojak, Aaron & Jill Davidson, Bob & Barbara Agdern, Cathy & Bob Wegrzyn, BioStrategics, John Supera, Ben & Shawna Murrie, Linda Zuckerman, Rhonda Golden and David & Julie Buchanan.

Most of all, thank *you*. Our hope is that, whether you are a Chicagoan or not, after reading this collection of stories about the place where we live and love, you will be inspired to tell your own.

Brian Golden & Cassy Sanders
Co-Coordinators, *The Chicago Landmark Project*

State & Madison: The Chicago Grid

By Marisa Wegrzyn

Copyright 2011 by Marisa Wegrzyn. All rights reserved. CAUTION: Professionals and amateurs are hereby warned that *State & Madison: The Chicago Grid* is subject to a royalty. They are fully protected by the copyright laws of the United States of America and of all countries covered by the international Copyright Union (included the Dominion of Canada and the rest of the British Commonwealth), the Berne Convention, the Pan-American Copyright Convention and the University Copyright Convention, as well as all rights, including professional and amateur stage rights, motion picture, recitation, lecturing, public reading, radio broadcasting, television, video or sound recording, all other forms of mechanical or electronic reproduction, such as CD-ROM, CD-I, DVD, information storage and retrieval systems and photocopying, and the rights of translation into foreign languages, are strictly reserved. Particular emphasis is laid upon the matter of readings, permission for which must be secured in writing.

Required royalties must be paid every time this play is performed before any audience, whether or not it is presented for profit and whether or not admission is charged. To obtain stock and amateur performance rights, you must contact:

> Morgan Jenness
> Abrams Artists Agency
> 275 Seventh Ave., 26th Floor
> New York, NY 10001
> 646-486-4600 x223
> Morgan.jenness@abramsartny.com

Playwright Biography
Marisa's plays include *Killing Women, Psalms of a Questionable Nature, Ten Cent Night, Hickorydickory,* and *Diversey Harbor.* Her black comedy *The Butcher of Baraboo* was produced in Steppenwolf Theatre's First Look Repertory in 2006, premiered Off Broadway at Second Stage in 2007, and published in the Smith & Kraus anthology New Playwrights: The Best Plays of 2008. Other theatres that have presented her work include Chicago Dramatists, Moxie Theatre in San Diego, Victory Theatre Center in Burbank, Actors Theatre of Louisville, Rivendell Theatre, Geva Theatre Center, Lucid by Proxy in Los Angeles, Washington University in St Louis, HotCity Theatre in St Louis, Nice People Theatre Company in Philadelphia, The Hourglass Group in NYC, Baltimore Centerstage, and The Magic Theatre in San Francisco. She is currently working on commissions from Steppenwolf and Yale Rep, and her writing was cited in The Chicago Reader's list, "Best of Chicago 2008." She received the 2009 Wendy Wasserstein Playwriting Prize for *Hickorydickory*. Marisa is a resident playwright at Chicago Dramatists, works as a mentor for high school playwrights as part of Pegasus Players Young Playwrights Festival, and is a founding member of Theatre Seven of Chicago.

Acknowledgments
State & Madison: The Chicago Grid premiered as part of The Chicago Landmark Project in June 2011. It was directed by Jennifer Green with the following cast:

EDWARD P. BRENNAN	Joe Zarrow
IRENE BRENNAN	Tracey Kaplan

Cast
EDWARD P. BRENNAN
IRENE BRENNAN

Setting
The Brennan's kitchen. A lake in Paw Paw, Michigan. State & Madison.

Time
1901

Joe Zarrow and Tracey Kaplan in *State & Madison: The Chicago Grid*

The Chicago Landmark Project
June – July, 2011
Produced by Theatre Seven of Chicago
Photo by Amanda Clifford

State & Madison: The Chicago Grid
by Marisa Wegrzyn

(Chicago, 1901. Edward P. Brennan is at a kitchen table covered in maps and street plans and a pile of books. Even more rolled maps on the floor. Irene Brennan is at the table with a cup of coffee and a plate of toast on the only bit of table top not covered by maps. Edward reads aloud his letter to the newspaper.)

EDWARD
"It would behoove our city to adopt uniform street numbering system, and designate State Street and Madison Street as the baseline, their intersection becoming zero East and West, and zero North and South. The new numbering system should indicate how far an address is from the State and Madison baselines, and odd and even numbers should be used to indicate the side of the street the residence or business is located. Currently, a man has to spend half his time studying street guides in order to be able to find his way around town. You may recall the saying "All roads lead to Rome." What if, in our city, all streets lead to State and Madison streets?" *(pause)* What do you think?

IRENE
Rome is a nice touch.

EDWARD
It's not too much?

IRENE
Rome is epic. It's good.

EDWARD
But...Rome burned down.

IRENE
Cities burn down, it happens.

EDWARD
Rome is too much it burned down and it's too much. Is it too much? It's too much. Would you mind checking the commas? *(He

gives her the letter. She looks it over.) This letter to the newspaper is only the beginning. There will be more letters. I'll write as many letters as it takes to rid this city of its nonsensical street numbering system based off the branches of a dirty, meandering river. Businesses will hate changing addresses.

IRENE
Stationery businesses? Stationery business will not hate you. They will love printing up new stationery for everybody. They will beat the drum for this idea. And map printers!

EDWARD
(dreamy) Map printers.

IRENE
The challenge, though, is it's a job for the City Council and you're…

EDWARD
A nobody.

IRENE
You're not on the City Council.

EDWARD
I'm a nobody.

IRENE
You are Edward Brennan, the best clerk that Lyon & Healy has ever had. And you are late for work.

(Edward looks at his watch. Oh shit, he's late.)

You'll want plenty of time to pack tonight, so if you can leave the office early, do.

EDWARD
Will you borrow an extra trunk from your brother?

IRENE
We're only packing the week.

EDWARD
For my maps and books.

IRENE
You want to haul these maps and books to Paw Paw?

EDWARD
And a couple of the books in my study. Two or three. Or ten. I promise no more than will fit in your brother's trunk.

IRENE
Fifty books would fit in that trunk.

EDWARD
Really? You think I could bring that many?

IRENE
Edward. I refuse to share your company with fifty books. Your hands will caress their pages delicately for hours, and how do you think that makes me feel? Watching from afar, wishing I had been born a book.

EDWARD
I have always admired your spine.

IRENE
This is the last summer we will have together, the two of us.

EDWARD
We'll have plenty more summers together.

IRENE
But the two of us, *alone*? We'll take the boat together. Talk about nothing and everything for hours the way we did when we were courting.

EDWARD
All right. No books.

IRENE
Of course you can bring *some* books. I'm not trying to ruin your life.

EDWARD
Irene, there is nothing you could do to ruin my life.

(Irene begins to clean up the table, ruining his life.)

STOP!!!! *(She stops.)* I'm sorry. Sorry. I'm sorry. I have things in a particular order.

IRENE
There's an order to this… *(mess)*?

EDWARD
There is a system.

IRENE
A system.

EDWARD
Yes.

IRENE
To the mess on the table there is a system.

EDWARD
Yes. I'm sorry. Yes. May I leave it for now?

IRENE
Mrs. Frick and the ladies from the church will be over this afternoon.

EDWARD

Tell Mrs Frick not to sit in my chair. Did you hear it crack last time she sat on it? Poor chair couldn't handle her hippo bottom. Let me clear this in a manner which suits my system.

(He can't decide where to start cleaning. He moves one thing and has anxiety.)

IRENE

Edward, you're late, go. I won't touch it. I promise. Mrs Frick is already critical of how I keep my house, what difference would a kitchen table full of confusion make. Go. And don't forget: home early to pack for Paw Paw.

(Edward exits the kitchen.)

I had been looking forward to leaving these hot streets behind. They'll be coming with us in rolled-up form, I suppose.

(Edward steps forward to address the audience. Irene sits in a row boat in a lake in Paw Paw, Michigan, waiting.)

EDWARD

(to audience) Here is what happened. Shortsightedness is what happened, you see. There are not one. Not two. But three separate systems of street numbering. As Chicago cannibalized adjacent communities, there were street name duplications. For god's sake, there are seventeen Lincoln streets, avenues, and places. I respect Abraham Lincoln as much as anyone, but the man is problematic on a street map. A nuisance. I am sorry, Mr. Lincoln, but I have to say it. And some streets go by multiple names. God help anyone who lives on Green Street, Lime Street, Dayton Street, Florence Avenue, Craft Street, Reta Avenue, and Newberry Avenue. That's one street! Seven names for one street! As if labeled by a madman. I'm surprised all the city's delivery men have not collectively hanged themselves.

IRENE

Will you help me row, Edward.

                        EDWARD
One minute.

                        IRENE
The mosquitoes are vicious! *(slaps at an insect)*

                        EDWARD
What sense does this make: The other day, I was to meet a man at an address on 22nd street in the south shore. At one moment I was at 550 E 22nd street, but just a few steps over the 22nd street bridge I was at 1 W 22nd street. And I won't even get started on South Water Street and North Water Street. *(beat)* The problem is they're parallel streets with completely different numbering! It's... it's just... *(can't express how crazy it is in words)*. I know I'm not the only one who wants to fix the problem. It can be fixed. That's why problems exist. Problems exist to be corrected.

(He gets in the rowboat. He rows.)

                        IRENE
It would be nice to own a cottage in Michigan. I would love to have a small place here, for the children to play and swim in the summer, away from the city. *(slaps insect)*

                        EDWARD
Not as many bugs in the city.

                        IRENE
I suppose not as many, no, but the smell is certainly better. And the quiet. It's nice. We'll be back dodging streetcars and horses soon enough.

                        EDWARD
I miss being trampled in the crush of humanity.

                        IRENE
Are you not relaxed at all?

                        EDWARD
I am... relaxing.

IRENE
(at his unhappiness) We can end our vacation early.

EDWARD
(an apology) Irene, no. I am far too relaxed. You've relaxed me too much. I'm done for. Might as well throw me overboard and let me float away.

IRENE
I'm not throwing you overboard. I need you to row me back to shore.

(They slap insects.)

IRENE and EDWARD
Got it!

IRENE
The Burkhardt's are building a summer home, not far from here. On a lake called Fish Lake.

EDWARD
Practical name for a lake.

IRENE
Of course you like that, Fish Lake, a lake filled with fish. Name it what it is. Like when we adopted the cat and you named her Kitty.

EDWARD
Kitty loves her name. Anybody who comes to the house already knows the cat's name. She purrs: "These strangers *know me*."

IRENE
I suppose we'll name our child Boy if it's a boy, or Girl if it's a girl?

EDWARD
I am happy with Charles or Mary, but whatever you wish.

IRENE
What would you think about a home here?

EDWARD
My income doesn't compare to John Burkhardt's bank manager salary.

IRENE
I'm not suggesting a summer home. A permanent home. A *home* home.

EDWARD
Here? In Michigan?

IRENE
Maybe not *here*, but away from Chicago.

EDWARD
(laughs, then realizing) ...You're serious. What would I do here? Chop wood? Hunt deer? These hands are not wood-chopping, deer-hunting hands, no, these are pencil-scribbling, paper-shuffling hands. I am not living in Michigan. No.

IRENE
You're acting like I suggested we live in *Wisconsin*.

EDWARD
How long have you been thinking this? Do you really want to move?

IRENE
The city is no place to raise children. It's dirty. It's dangerous. When I was a child—

EDWARD
—you rode horses and swung from ropes into rivers and had a delightfully bucolic upbringing.

IRENE
(with a "don't make fun" tone) Edward.

EDWARD
Chicago is our home. Where my work is.

IRENE
Smaller towns need good accountants.

EDWARD
I am not talking about my work at Lyon & Healy.

IRENE
Ah. Your grid system. Your plan for the city, for the lives of thousands and thousands of strangers. A plan for *their* convenience, for *their* lives.

(a beat)

We ought to return to shore.

(Edward rows.)

I had a terrible dream about zero. On your street grid.

EDWARD
You had a terrible dream about Madison and State Street?

IRENE
I don't want to talk about it.

EDWARD
All right.

IRENE
(she really wants to talk about it) In my dream I was shopping, and I had just bought a rocking horse covered in strawberry jam from a shopkeeper who was actually Father Donald wearing a Viking helmet, and when I crossed the intersection of Madison and State with the strawberry jam rocking horse, the street gave way to a sink hole that swallowed me, and the rocking horse burst into flames, and then I woke up.

EDWARD
I see.

IRENE
Why not have the center of your grid system be one instead of zero?

EDWARD
What has that to do with a rocking horse covered in strawberry jam?

IRENE
Edward, it was *on fire*.

EDWARD
It was a dream.

IRENE
The number one instead of the number zero would allow me to sleep better.

EDWARD
If a person wants to calculate the number of miles from the center point of a grid, zero makes sense. It's zero. Zero east-west, Zero north-south.

IRENE
You have created this thing with a point of non-existence at its center, that's all.

EDWARD
Zero exists. Zero is a number.

IRENE
I know it's a number, but it's also nothing.

EDWARD
Zero is mathematics and god is in mathematics, I am certain of that. Maybe what you're feeling is a superstitious thing. Like the number thirteen. Or stepping on a crack.

IRENE
It's a lonely thing, zero. Like…I'm not sure. Like… the way you can be surrounded by thousands of people and feel so alone.

EDWARD
Do you feel alone? *(a pause)* Why do you feel so alone? Why?

IRENE
I don't know.

(A moment – he invites her out of the rowboat. As if showing her around his city, a streetscape imagined. Maybe there will be city sounds, maybe not.)

EDWARD
Imagine standing on the corner of State and Madison. It's a beautiful Saturday afternoon in September. You have just been shopping at Marshall Field, and not for a rocking horse covered in strawberry jam.

IRENE
Did I buy those shoes I wanted?

EDWARD
Um.

IRENE
The shoes I wanted for Christmas but you couldn't afford.

EDWARD
I still can't afford them.

IRENE
I can understand you can't afford a summer home, but a pair of shoes?

EDWARD
What's wrong with the shoes in your closet?

IRENE
Edward, this is my imagination.

EDWARD
All right. You bought those shoes. And a mink. And a necklace with diamonds.

IRENE
I'm glad you realize we are exceedingly wealthy in our imaginations.

EDWARD
With plenty leftover to build a summer home.

IRENE
Yes! All right. I like this. I have stepped out with my shoes, mink, and necklace, and Edward, watch out for the—

(Edward steps in horse poop.)

EDWARD
Oh, horses! *(scrapes shoe)*

IRENE
(Irene "poop is funny" Brennan) Poop…All right, so, we have walked south to State and Madison, yes?

EDWARD
The people on the sidewalk, the hustle and bustle, street cars and carriages going north and south. Humanity pulses around you. Look at your feet in your beautiful new shoes, the shoes you love, and the ground below your feet. Miraculously, there's no street traffic, so you cross the intersection diagonally to step on the exact center.

IRENE
Don't make me do it.

                    EDWARD
I'm not going to shove you into an imagined oblivion. I'm right
next to you. And our child, he or she is there too. Charles or Mary.

                    IRENE
Kitty is a nice name.

(Edward makes sure she's joking – she is.)

                    EDWARD
And now you're thinking about stepping onto the zero, yes? It's
right there. The center of the entire city of Chicago. The point
from which all existence radiates forth. Our zero at State and
Madison… a city is born. If you know that point, cradled between
mountains of buildings, you will never be lost. The entire city of
Chicago is yours. And ours. And we are all here, together.

(a moment)

Ready?

                    IRENE
Ready.

(They step on zero east-west, Zero north-south, State & Madison. End play.)

Lincoln & Webster: Oz Park

By The Red Orchid Youth Ensemble

Copyright 2011 by A Red Orchid Theatre. All rights reserved.
CAUTION: Professionals and amateurs are hereby warned that *Lincoln & Webster: Oz Park* is subject to a royalty. They are fully protected by the copyright laws of the United States of America and of all countries covered by the international Copyright Union (included the Dominion of Canada and the rest of the British Commonwealth), the Berne Convention, the Pan-American Copyright Convention and the University Copyright Convention, as well as all rights, including professional and amateur stage rights, motion picture, recitation, lecturing, public reading, radio broadcasting, television, video or sound recording, all other forms of mechanical or electronic reproduction, such as CD-ROM, CD-I, DVD, information storage and retrieval systems and photocopying, and the rights of translation into foreign languages, are strictly reserved. Particular emphasis is laid upon the matter of readings, permission for which must be secured in writing.

Required royalties must be paid every time this play is performed before any audience, whether or not it is presented for profit and whether or not admission is charged. To obtain stock and amateur performance rights, you must contact:

A Red Orchid Theatre
Kirsten@aredorchidtheatre.org

Playwright Biography

The Red Orchid Youth Ensemble was the natural outgrowth of A Red Orchid Theatre's first all youth production in 2009, *A Very Merry Unauthorized Scientology Pageant* by Alex Timbers and Kyle Jarrow, directed by Steve Wilson and AROT ensemble member, Lance Baker. Under the direction of founders Steve Wilson and Larry Grimm, the youth ensemble began with a series of classes on scene study, clowning, improv, on-camera workshops, and the business of acting which led to in-house workshop productions, appearances in Collaboraction's *Sketchbook* two years running, Theatre Seven of Chicago's *The Chicago Landmark Project* and a successful production of Homer's *The Iliad* adapted by ensemble member Craig Wright and directed by Steve Wilson. The mission of the youth ensemble is to produce theatre which reflects the narrative complexity and authentic voices of its young members who will be the theatrical visionaries of tomorrow.

Acknowledgments

Lincoln & Webster: Oz Park premiered as part of The Chicago Landmark Project in June 2011. It was directed by Lawrence Grimm and assistant directed by Elise Lammers with the following cast:

DOROTHY #1:	Alina Taber
DOROTHY #2:	Eden Strong
DOROTHY #3:	Elenna Sindler
DOROTHY #4:	Elita Ernsteen
DOROTHY #5:	Kara Ryan
DOROTHY #6:	Jaiden Fallo Sauter

Cast
DOROTHY #1
DOROTHY #2
DOROTHY #3
DOROTHY #4
DOROTHY #5
DOROTHY #6

Setting
Oz Park.

Time
Now.

Elenna Sindler, Elita Ernsteen, Alina Taber, Eden Strong and Jaiden Fallo Sauter in *Lincoln & Webster: Oz Park*

The Chicago Landmark Project
June – July, 2011
Produced by Theatre Seven of Chicago
Photo by Amanda Clifford

Lincoln & Webster: Oz Park
By The Red Orchid Youth Ensemble

Prologue

(We hear an audio montage of Youth Ensemble voices, Oz Park visitors and characters from "The Wizard of Oz" in black out. Lights up to reveal multiple entrances on Youth Ensemble members with brooms in hand for RUBY SLIPPER BROOM DANCE.

Scene One: Questions Asked

ALINA
Spring 2011, Oz Park on a sunny day.

EDEN
We are definitely not in Kansas anymore Dorothy.

ELITA
But we are not too far from home either.

JAIDEN
A block away…an intersection where reality meets fantasy.

KARA
We followed the yellow brick road.

ELENNA
And this is what we wanted to know from the wizards.

(Using the brooms as microphones, in a single file line, the actors ask as if interviewing the audience.)

ALINA
If you had to choose between

EDEN
heart,

ELITA
brains,

JAIDEN
or courage,

ALINA
which would you choose and why?

EDEN
How do you feel when you stand next to the Tin Man?

ELITA
What is the most courageous thing you have ever done?

KARA
What do you fear most?

JAIDEN
Why do bad things happen to good people?

ELENNA
What is your Oz?

ALINA
Has your heart ever been broken?

ELITA
Have you ever broken a heart?

JAIDEN
Define the word home.

(Ensemble takes a step forward and freezes in the shared line.)

ENSEMBLE
Why is there no place like home?

Scene Two: I Am Heart

(Actors create a heart portrait and break out of it when they have a line.)

      ENSEMBLE
I am heart

      ELENNA
I am from deep within your soul.

      ALINA
I am strongest when I am whole,

      ELITA
…*you* are strongest when you follow me.

      KARA
Sometimes I worry that I am not good at what I do.

      ELITA
When no one sees me, I feel like taking a break from the teenager years and switching bodies.

      JAIDEN
Heart…that is the most constant thing. You can lose your brain, you can lose your courage, but you wanna keep your heart.

      EDEN
Have you ever broken a heart?

      JAIDEN
Yeah…when I only had a brain.

      KARA
Do we have to say how recently?

      ALINA
(*masculine*) Yes, I would assume that I have broken someone's heart.

ELITA
I did…I laughed madly in front of someone who had just asked me to marry him.

ELENNA
I'm not sure that I have, but if there is someone out there…I am so sorry.

ENSEMBLE
I am Heart

ALINA
I am strongest when I am whole,

ELITA
…*you* are strongest when you follow me.

(*During the following, the ensemble uses the brooms in a percussive beat to simulate the heart beat.*)

EDEN
When I am on the waterslide…..my heart stops. (*1 broom beat*)
I see the water below me. (*2 broom beats and movement*)
I feel the water pressure behind me. (*3 broom beats and movement*)
I feel my heart skip a beat. (*4 broom beats with one skip and movement*)
A rush of adrenaline. (*rapid fire broom beats*)
My heart is beating way too fast to be normal. (*movement*)
We are leaving Timber Ridge Lodge and I ask my dad if I can go on the waterslide one last time. He says:

ALINA
O.k.…but hurry up.

KARA
Yeah let's go! You are cutting in on my twitter time.

EDEN
I thought I was prepared to swim but the current pushed faster and went:

                    ELITA/ALINA/ELENNA/KARA/JAIDEN
No you don't!

                              EDEN
I was just like:

                    ELITA/ALINA/ELENNA/KARA/JAIDEN
What?

                              EDEN
The water was about four feet but at the time I was 3 feet and 10 inches. I tried to clear my way to the surface and I don't know how long I was down there but eventually I lost consciousness. A lifeguard came to rescue me, I found myself lying on a floatation device coughing. I felt like my heart leapt out of my throat.

Scene Three: I Am Courage

(Actors create an opening courage portrait, possibly introducing or reintroducing ruby slippers.)

                              ELITA
I am courage.

                              KARA
I am from a place where everyone is a close being.

                              JAIDEN
I may seem inspired but I am also confused, especially when I have….

                            ENSEMBLE
FEAR! *(single file line)*

                              ELITA
What do you fear most?

                              EDEN
Spiders.

                    ELENNA
Sharks.

                    ALINA
Heights.

                    JAIDEN
Loneliness.

                    KARA
Interviews….and young white men.

                    ALINA
I am courage. When it comes to seeing new faces and exploring unknown worlds, I am brave, gentle and curious.

                    EDEN
What is the most courageous thing you have done?

                    ELITA
Being a mom.

                    ELENNA
Walking my dog….. in the park…at night.

                    JAIDEN
Going through eight surgeries.

                    EDEN
Killing a spider with my watch.

                    ALINA
You can lose courage! (*As Alina yells this, the ensemble scurries to respective spots, Alina crosses over to bench.*) I was sitting in my family room. My friend had come over

                    JAIDEN
…to stay the weekend.

ALINA
We were sitting together...not really socializing. Our minds focused and slowly being drained by

ALINA & JAIDEN
the big LED screen in front of us.

ALINA
I had pulled out a white Mac laptop and waited for the dark screen to turn bright. I checked my Facebook and my friend asked...

JAIDEN
....if I could check mine?

ALINA
She started talking to her friends. Some that I knew...

JAIDEN
...some that you didn't.

ALINA
I told her to say "hi" to one of her friends for me..

JAIDEN
..and right when she did....

ALINA & JAIDEN
(*shocked*) A MESSAGE APPEARED ON THE SCREEN!

ELITA
(*abstracted computer with broom*) "You dumb BLEEP!"

EDEN
"You should kill yourself you BLEEP."

ELITA & EDEN
"I HATE YOU!"

ALINA
I read this with absolute shock and disbelief. And I asked her, "Why did he say that?"

JAIDEN
Oh, I'm sure it's my sister. Here, let me check.

(Quickly and sneakily Eden and Elita push their arms through an arriving Kara and Elenna and sing ala munchkins "We represent the cyber bully guild, the cyber bully guild.")

ALINA
She acted like she didn't mind it, although I did.

JAIDEN
(typing) Sis...is that you?

KARA
This isn't your sister you dumb BLEEP!

ELENNA
You are a stupid_____

(Ensemble chimes in one at a time in a chorus of the word "Bleep" holding onto the "ee" sound as a group but all landing on a unified "eep!")

(Beat.)

ALINA
I stared at her *(she does for a beat)*...and grabbed the laptop. I began to type back to him but she –

JAIDEN
took it away and said, "No, don't".

ALINA
I told her...

KARA
You can't just sit there.

                    ELENNA
Are you o.k.?

                    EDEN
I'm sorry.

                    ELITA
He's such a jerk.

                    ALINA
I love you, and he has no right to say those things. He is most definitely a bad witch!

                    JAIDEN
What?

                    ALINA
I wanted so badly to tell him how much of a jerk he was but I let her

                    JAIDEN
...do what she wanted.

                    ALINA
I saw the sadness swell up in her..

                    JAIDEN
..though it never came out. *(Beat.)* She hid her feelings,

                    ALINA
and looking back on it I should have been courageous enough to take charge of the situation and stick up for her.

                    EDEN
I know I have a heart, because I can feel it breaking.

                    JAIDEN
(Out of character and scene slightly, with gentle compassion.) Surrender Dorothy.

ELITA
(to Alina, consoling.) Pay no attention to the man behind the curtain.

(Alina is reconciled and partially soothed.)

ENSEMBLE
I am courage.

Scene Four: I Am Brains

ENSEMBLE
I am Brains.

ELITA
You can thank me for every decision you have ever made.

JAIDEN
(with cocky arrogance) Like when you have heart and courage? That was my idea. Me...the brainiac.

ALINA
I am strongest when I am alone but not lonely.

ENSEMBLE
I am brains.

ELENNA
I am strongest when I help people be better people. Like when I stop them from doing something wrong.

EDEN
Which would you choose?

KARA
I would choose a brain - so I could think of how to get a heart and courage and everything else. See? I'm smart.

ALINA
Tough one. You need brains to have a good head on your shoulders but if you're not compassionate you aren't anything.

ELENNA
To be smart in the world really, really helps, you can figure out how to have heart, be courageous, you can even find.... your OZ.

EDEN
What is your Oz?

ELENNA
Writing.

JAIDEN
Anywhere I can worship God....

KARA
Um...I got nothing.

ALINA
To write a novel...

ELITA
To sit on the beach after she writes the novel.

EDEN
America is Oz.

KARA
Chicago. Chicago is my Oz.

EDEN
But how do you get there? (*Defiant as if to the wizard*)

ELITA
(*good Glinda like*) Follow the yellow brick road.

              KARA
We tried that, there's nothing but like a Dairy Queen, an abandoned hospital and college bars.

              ALINA
Wish upon a star.

              ENSEMBLE
Not.

              ALINA
(*short transition*) Spring 2011, Oz Park on a sunny day.

              EDEN
We are definitely not in Kansas anymore Dorothy.

              ELITA
But we are not too far from home either.

              JAIDEN
A block away…an intersection where reality definitely met fantasy.

              KARA
We followed the yellow brick road.

              ELENNA
(*very Mickey Mouse Club, thrilled with the discovery*) ….and look at where it led spontaneously with no warning whatsoever?

(*A very official looking cardboard box complete with a Chicago city seal is labeled: "Magic Chicago Slippers. Dream at your own risk!"*)

              ELENNA
(*digging*) Check it out…(*she pulls ruby slippers out of box to excited glee from the group. They start to put on the slippers and find instructions inside each slipper.*)

              ENSEMBLE
(*They initially read cautiously and with judgment.*) There's no place like…. Chicago?

(But then, each time they repeat with more commitment and heightening, closing their eyes and really trying.)

(Ensemble repeats phrase until almost frenzied: "There's no place like Chicago." When actors are at fever pitch the final sound cue montage kicks in, temporary dim or blackout, then at sound cue's sharp crescendo, lights full up. Ensemble freezes. Stunned. Wide-eyed. Ensemble backs turn so that shirts read "HOME". Ensemble lets out an exhale. Blackout. End play.)

Garfield & State: Midway Liquors

By J. Nicole Brooks

Copyright 2011 by J. Nicole Brooks. All rights reserved. CAUTION: Professionals and amateurs are hereby warned that *Garfield & State: Midway Liquors* is subject to a royalty. They are fully protected by the copyright laws of the United States of America and of all countries covered by the international Copyright Union (included the Dominion of Canada and the rest of the British Commonwealth), the Berne Convention, the Pan-American Copyright Convention and the University Copyright Convention, as well as all rights, including professional and amateur stage rights, motion picture, recitation, lecturing, public reading, radio broadcasting, television, video or sound recording, all other forms of mechanical or electronic reproduction, such as CD-ROM, CD-I, DVD, information storage and retrieval systems and photocopying, and the rights of translation into foreign languages, are strictly reserved. Particular emphasis is laid upon the matter of readings, permission for which must be secured in writing.

Required royalties must be paid every time this play is performed before any audience, whether or not it is presented for profit and whether or not admission is charged. To obtain stock and amateur performance rights, you must contact:

> J. Nicole Brooks
> nicbrooks@me.com
> Amaryliss Seabrooks, Legal Representative
> Amaryliss9@yahoo.com

Playwright Biography

J. Nicole Brooks is a theatre practitioner with credits in acting, directing and writing. She is author to *Black Diamond: The Years The Locusts Have Eaten*, *Fedra Queen of Haiti*, *Kamala Masterclass*, and *Shotgun Harriet*. Awards include the 2010 Black Theatre Alliance Award Best Actress in a Play for *Fedra Queen of Haiti*, 2008 LA Ovation Best Featured Actress in a Play for Paul Oakley Stovall's *As Much As You Can*. Her comedic blog www.doctaslick.blogspot.com was named to the top 100 blogs in LA by global media editors Sparkah.com. In 2009 she was awarded the prestigious Theatre Communications Group Fox Foundation Resident Actor Fellowship. She is a daughter of Chicago's South Side, a fan of the White Sox and proud alumna of Northern Illinois University School of Theatre & Dance. She is an ensemble member of the Tony Award-winning Lookingglass Theatre Company of Chicago, and an associate of Collaboraction Theatre Company.

Acknowledgments

Garfield & State: Midway Liquors premiered as part of The Chicago Landmark Project in June 2011. It was directed by Jonathan Green with the following cast:

MARAUD	Cameron Miller
SOCAL HIPSTER	Adrian Snow
HER FRIEND	Paloma Nozicka

Garfield & State: Midway Liquors

Cast

MARAUD, Mid 20s – 30s. Charming, intelligent, quick-witted, native Chicagoan

SOCAL HIPSTER, 20s. Attractive, mysterious, open spirit. An Angelino.

HER FRIEND, 20s. Ultra hip, snarky, total kid sister. An Angelino.

Setting

State Street at Lake Street, the northwest corner near the ABC studios.

Time

Downtown Chicago on a warm spring day.

Garfield & State: Midway Liquors

Cameron Miller and Adrian Snow in *Garfield & State: Midway Liquors*

The Chicago Landmark Project
June – July, 2011
Produced by Theatre Seven of Chicago
Photo by Amanda Clifford

Garfield & State: Midway Liquors
by J. Nicole Brooks

(SoCal and Her Friend carry typical tourist shopping bags which include Garrett Popcorn, Art Institute of Chicago, and other local boutiques. Her Friend wears huge designer sunglasses and is always preoccupied by her smart phone. She is always underwhelmed and way too cool to be bothered with anything.)

(Maraud sketches in his book, a larger sketchbook. He takes notice of the pair. SoCal looks into a Chicago Tourist Attraction Handbook.)

SOCAL
Ooh! I saw on the Cooking Channel that Lou Malnati's has good deep dish! Wanna?

HER FRIEND
Dude no. I was just looking at my abs earlier -- The worst. If you can't look straight down and see your pubes? Too fat. Ok -- Jeff just texted me. *(reading)* He wants to meet us in the lobby and get drinks at the hotel bar. Why does Karly keep texting photos of her kid? Its like Jesus, we get it. You like your baby.

SOCAL
I swear you're one of the worst people I know.

(Maraud swoops in.)

MARAUD
(about her bags) Hope you got a tin of popcorn for me.

SOCAL
Oh. Hi you again! Nice to see you.

(SoCal totally digs this dude. And he digs her. "They're the only two people in the room".)

HER FRIEND
No no nonono. Because see -- you did that drawing of us yesterday, and totally made me look like I had Rosacea. I know you

people here in the middle states don't get sun, but I do not have blotchy skin.

SOCAL
(*Shooting daggers with her eyes at Her Friend*) Go over there.

(*Her Friend continues playing on the phone, just a few feet away. Still giving the side eye and maintaining a supersonic ear.*)

MARAUD
See you been all over the Magnificent Mile. You visit the Southside like I suggested?

SOCAL
Sorry. Nothing in my tourist bible lists the South side. See Wrigley, Willis Tower --

MARAUD
Pump your breaks baby girl, that there is blaspheme. *Sears Tower*. Now does your "bible" mention the wonders of South Chicago?

SOCAL
Nope.

MARAUD
May I?

(*He flips through and makes it up as he goes along.*)

Says right here that the south side is worthy of exploration. You can see remnants of the 1893 World Fair, DuSable Museum, White Sox Park, the Obama residence... And it says you can see the Washington Park neighborhood--the childhood 'hood of your future husband.

SOCAL
And what about my deep dish pizza?

MARAUD
Deep dish? Girl it's the South Side. We got pizza puffs. Cheese and tomato paste wrapped in dough--then deep fried. You can't get that epicurean goodness downtown.

SOCAL
So you're an artist *and* a ghetto tour guide?

MARAUD
No baby, I'm a time lord. Like Dr. Who. I've come to take you on an adventure.

(SoCal is amused. Her Friend is over it.)

HER FRIEND
Okay, I'm trying to give a fuck about your conversation, but it's just too weird. Can we go?

SOCAL
(covering) Pretty day out. Finally the weather is like...well it's better than when we first got here.

MARAUD
Give it 15 minutes, it'll change.

SOCAL
What you don't like it warm? Thought you Chicagoans were sick of the cold.

MARAUD
We do...but see, when you're down here warm weather is great. But when you go south of Chinatown or west of the United Center...weather makes it another story. When it get hot, they shoot.

SOCAL
Who is they?

MARAUD
Your cousins.

SOCAL
My cousins?

MARAUD
Sorry to break it to you, but when the weather breaks, people get buck, crime spikes. Brothers like to shoot.

HER FRIEND
(explaining to SoCal) He means it's like June Gloom in LA. You know how the Marine layer is totally depressing? It's like kill go yourself.

SOCAL
I mean if the cops know people shoot when it's hot, why don't they, use more cops? Or use a dude like the one from that show Numb3rs?

MARAUD
Well, they do some kind of predictions...its simple mathematics...actually it's statistics. Linear Regression. So they basically gather data to make predictions --

HER FRIEND
And that's my cue to exit. Going back to the hotel for a little smut and hair pulling, with Jeff. You two can play Sherman and Mr. Peabody with your -- time travel. Call me if you get shot.

(She takes the bags. Tosses hair. Exits.)

SOCAL
So where's our Tardis, doctor?

MARAUD
You're accepting my invitation?

SOCAL
Not without knowing your name.

MARAUD

Maraud.

SOCAL

Maraud. Like a thief?

MARAUD

My mother wanted to name me Prometheus, and even though it was Greek, she thought it sounded too ghetto. So.

SOCAL

Wow. Ok.
I'm Persephone.

MARAUD

And you had the nerve to trip on my name?

SOCAL

What can I say, my parents smoked a lot of pot.

MARAUD

Well then, Persephone. Looks like it's time for me to take you back to Hades.

(He extends his hand. She has a moment of hesitation.)

MARAUD

All aboard.

SOCAL

I don't...um...

MARAUD

Come on. What are you afraid of? Traveling time and space is easy. Knowing that we can't alter the past to save the future...that's the hard part.

SOCAL
Okay, I enjoy Octavia Butler and sci-fi like the next girl. But I do know that the laws of physics will not allow "backwards" travel in time.

MARAUD
I beg to differ--it is currently *unknown* whether the laws of physics will allow such travel.

SOCAL
Okay then smart ass. Make me a liar. Take me back to the past.

(She accepts his hand. Sound and lights. The city passes them in a peripheral, theatrical way...it goes from the sounds of a bustling city to a barren soundscape. These are moments of time travel. They arrive.)

SOCAL
Are we? Where are we?

MARAUD
The neighborhood of Washington Park.

SOCAL
(she observes passersby and the surroundings) I didn't even know they made that kind of car anymore, my dad had that same car when -- I was little. Are...high top fades back in style? Wait...where are we?

MARAUD
We went from State Street "that great street", down the black belt passing the Robert Taylor projects to this corner right here. Garfield, 55th & State. On the northwest corner we have Pizza King -- they sell pizza, northeast is the Butternut bread factory, yummy doughy goodness...southeast we have Kentucky Fried Chicken -- before it was KFC and here on the southwest corner is Midway Liquors. A place that will prove itself an effective center for the most trifling and lazy assed nword's. A few years from now in 2008 the FBI will label this intersection "one of the most dangerous corners in America."

Garfield & State: Midway Liquors

SOCAL
What do you mean a few years from now?

(SoCal is stunned. Maraud begins to write equations into his sketch pad.)

SOCAL
??? Oh my god -- did you roofie me -

MARAUD
The temperature for May 27, 1995 is 97 degrees -

SOCAL
MARAUD! This isn't funny. I'm scared --

MARAUD
I haven't drugged you. I assure you, you're in no danger.

SOCAL
It couldn't be 1995 -- it's 2011.

MARAUD
Suspend your disbelief and live in this moment.

SOCAL
I --

MARAUD
I won't let anything happen to you. I just have to figure this out. Go with it.

SOCAL
We're obviously shrooming so, I may as well enjoy the trip.

MARAUD
I wanted to run Linear Regression to see if I could explore why this corner fell victim to the crime. Things never developed here.

SOCAL
That's what happens in big cities. Areas go from good to bad. Bad to good. Hey maybe you'll get lucky, replace the liquor store with a doggy bed and breakfast.

MARAUD
The tragedy of this place isn't some bloody massacre, or a 4 alarm fire. But the demise has been slow. So many factors at play...It just occurred to me that time displacement is also something to consider.

SOCAL
What's that?

MARAUD
Basically it's when new forms of activities replace another -- and it affects society. So dig it, take technology...kids used to go outside and play right--now they stay indoors and play video games. Television had an impact because it shifted people from going outside to the movies; the internet definitely affects face to face time...everybody is locked indoors and don't give a fuck about what's happening outdoors. They don't care about what's happening around them, because they're distracted by their own technology. Most people don't know their neighbors anymore.

SOCAL
So you're saying Facebook is the fall of mankind? Social networking destroyed the ghetto.

MARAUD
Ha. You funny. We're all distracted. This place used to be... This is where I grew up. I cut my teeth in the art world here. Simply observing the world, from this corner. The projects lined up State Street for as far as the eye could see -- that's how I learned perspective. When church let out, all the sisters with their hats on? Well that's how I learned about color. When I was little, there used to be this graffiti sprayed all over place. I don't mean gang signs either. It said things like "Free Fred Hampton Jr." and "Cain Killed Abel." I didn't get it at first. But as the years rolled by and the bullshit grew, I started to catch on.

                    SOCAL
What happens here?

                    MARAUD
We stop paying attention is what happens. We stopped connecting.
I could run linear regression...I could use all kinds of social science
but it won't change anything. There's nothing I can do.
The brother that owned the newsstand over there? Mr. Roy. He
used to save me some magazines and newspapers that he couldn't
sell, because he knew I liked to draw. He told me that I couldn't be
an artist unless I knew what was happening in the world. The
bakery. Man, you could smell that fresh baked bread for miles and
miles. The smell of that bread meant people were working, you
know. Even this liquor store here had fresh produce and a deli,
butcher and all. See we didn't have any grocery stores over here
really, so Midway was it. And the owners, a family, kept pretty
nice. I'd sit on the counter while my mother chatted with
them...they'd slide me a Blow Pop and drill me about my grades
and school. They were the pride of this neighborhood...and as
time went on, their fortune grew and they became millionaires...I'm
not kidding. Black millionaires at a time where they really could
have helped with development over here. But they just stacked
those papers; surrounding businesses failed...and this place
harbored all kinds of criminal behavior. I ain't saying a liquor store
could've saved us, but I feel like these cats turned a blind eye.
Aiding and abetting drug deals. Drug use. They stopped paying
attention.

(He takes a can of spray paint out of his bag. He shakes it)

                    MARAUD
Wanna know the worst part about this corner? Is that nothing
happens here. I mean nothing is forward moving. The bread
factory closed. Newsstand closed. KFC ain't goin nowhere. And so
neither is this liquor store. Churches, liquor stores, and nail shops--
that's what we have in the 'hood.

(He starts to shake the can.)

SOCAL

Look, I know you think that these guys are like the Khmer Rouge, but I seriously doubt vandalizing a liquor store will do anything.

(He sprays "CAIN KILLED ABEL".)

SOCAL

Okay. What now?

MARAUD

I don't know.

SOCAL

Maybe we can time travel to Watts. How about Detroit?

MARAUD

Yeah and lets add Gary, Indiana to the list.
But before we go solving all of the world's problems, I believe I owe you a pizza puff.
And hell, since it's 1995 I might as well treat you to a bottle of peach Boones Farm.

SOCAL

Step off, I'm a Zima girl.

(He extends his hand. She smiles, then takes it. Lights. Sound. End play.)

Ohio & The Lake: Navy Pier

By Robert Koon

Copyright 2011 by Robert Koon. All rights reserved. CAUTION: Professionals and amateurs are hereby warned that *Ohio & The Lake: Navy Pier* is subject to a royalty. They are fully protected by the copyright laws of the United States of America and of all countries covered by the international Copyright Union (included the Dominion of Canada and the rest of the British Commonwealth), the Berne Convention, the Pan-American Copyright Convention and the University Copyright Convention, as well as all rights, including professional and amateur stage rights, motion picture, recitation, lecturing, public reading, radio broadcasting, television, video or sound recording, all other forms of mechanical or electronic reproduction, such as CD-ROM, CD-I, DVD, information storage and retrieval systems and photocopying, and the rights of translation into foreign languages, are strictly reserved. Particular emphasis is laid upon the matter of readings, permission for which must be secured in writing.

Required royalties must be paid every time this play is performed before any audience, whether or not it is presented for profit and whether or not admission is charged. To obtain stock and amateur performance rights, you must contact:

Robert Koon
www.robertkoon.com

Playwright Biography
Robert Koon is a resident playwright at Chicago Dramatists, where he also serves as the company dramaturg. Chicago Dramatists produced his play *St. Colm's Inch* and published his play *Vintage Red and the Dust of the Road* (Joseph Jefferson Award Citation for New Work, American Theatre Critics Steinberg Award nominee) in their anthology *New Plays from Chicago*. Robert's other work includes *Odin's Horse* (Joseph Jefferson Award nominee), *The Point of Honor*, *Changing Attire*, *Solstice*, and *Looking West from Fira*. His newest play, *Menorca*, was produced at 16th Street Theatre in the fall of 2010. He is a member of The Dramatists Guild of America. He received his MFA from The University of California at Davis, and currently resides in Chicago with his wife, Jean Marie.

Acknowledgments
Ohio & The Lake: Navy Pier premiered as part of The Chicago Landmark Project in June 2011. It was directed by Brian Stojak with the following cast:

FATHER	Tim Curtis
DAUGHTER	Baize Buzan

Ohio & The Lake: Navy Pier

Cast
FATHER
DAUGHTER

Setting
The eastern end of Navy Pier.

Time
An afternoon in mid-August.

Baize Buzan and Tim Curtis in *Ohio & The Lake: Navy Pier*

The Chicago Landmark Project
June – July, 2011
Produced by Theatre Seven of Chicago
Photo by Amanda Clifford

Ohio & The Lake: Navy Pier
by Robert Koon

(The eastern end of Navy Pier. A summer day in mid-August. Sunny, hot. Father and Daughter sit looking out at the water. A plane flies overhead, an airliner headed east. She looks up and watches it.)

FATHER
So. All ready?

DAUGHTER
(Still watching the plane.) Oh. Yeah. I guess.

FATHER
What are you going to do with your car?

DAUGHTER
Leave it. Living on campus, who needs a car?

FATHER
Smart.

DAUGHTER
Yeah. Mom wanted me to take it. Said we could tow it. Roger said that wouldn't work.

FATHER
Probably not.
So are they both going, or just your mom?

DAUGHTER
Oh, Roger's going to drive. Which is just as good, because she's just going to cry.

FATHER
Yeah, probably.

DAUGHTER
She cries all the time. "My baby's going away."

FATHER
She's going to miss you.

DAUGHTER
She bought a web cam. She wants to Skype.

FATHER
Smart.

DAUGHTER
Whatever.

(They sit in silence.)

FATHER
So—

DAUGHTER
Why Navy Pier?

FATHER
What?

DAUGHTER
Why did we come to Navy Pier? I mean, Navy Pier. A tourist mall, for God's sake. That's where you want to come for our last day?

FATHER
We always used to come to Navy Pier before school started.

DAUGHTER
We always used to go to the Children's Museum, too. When I was, like, eight.

(Pause.)

FATHER
So, you're not going to want to ride the Ferris wheel, then.

(Eye roll from Daughter. Pause.)

I used to come out here before it was a mall. Quiet. Read the Sunday paper.
Before you were born.

(They sit. Another plane flies overhead. She watches it.)

DAUGHTER
I wish I could fly.

FATHER
Me, too. Sure make commuting easier.

DAUGHTER
I mean to Philadelphia.

FATHER
Oh.

DAUGHTER
Just get there, you know? Just get there and get on with it. All this…the big production. Moving. I should just take the car and do it myself.

(Father laughs.)

What, you don't think I could?

FATHER
I'm sure you could.

DAUGHTER
Pack the car, drive, unpack the car, done.

FATHER
Yep.

DAUGHTER
But there's all this big thing about it.

FATHER
Well, you know, Penn…Ivy League. It is a big thing.

DAUGHTER
Yeah, right. I mean moving. You know, people do this all the time.

FATHER
Yes. People do this all the time. But that doesn't matter. Not to me, not to your mom. You do not do this all the time. You are doing this for the first time, and so…it is a big thing. For us.

DAUGHTER
Well, yeah, for you.

FATHER
We're proud of you.

(No response.)

I'm proud of you. You're going to do fine.

DAUGHTER
Yeah.
You keep saying that like you're trying to convince yourself.

(Silence.)

FATHER
They used to actually dock ships here. Navy ships. They used to train pilots, right out there in the lake. To land on aircraft carriers. They took these ships and put the decks on them so they could practice.

(No response.)

They'd dock them right here and there would be, like, this whole Air and Water show right out there, all the time. *(Points at the lake.)* There's wrecks out there. In the lake. Planes. Landing on an aircraft carrier, you know, it's something you have to get right the first time, but you can't always get it right the first time, so…

(Makes the noise of a plane splashing into the lake.)

And the Navy, the Navy says that no one can salvage the planes because they're military equipment. 70 years in the lake. Like they're classified or something.

(No response.)

You never think about that. That there are all these wrecked planes out there.

(Pause.)

DAUGHTER
Did they die?

FATHER
What?

DAUGHTER
The pilots. You know. *(Mimics his plane-crashing noise.)* Did they die?

FATHER
I don't know. I suppose. Crashing a plane, kind of a serious thing.

DAUGHTER
One little mistake.

FATHER
Yeah. One little mistake. And it wasn't even like they were in the war yet.

DAUGHTER
And let that be a lesson to us all.

FATHER
What?

DAUGHTER
Let that be a lesson to us all. One little mistake, and there you are, drowning in the lake. You're not even in the war yet, but there you are. Drowning in the lake. One little mistake, and you're drowning in the lake. Ya-dadda-dadda-da-da.
"A parable from Dad, to his daughter leaving for college."

(Beat.)

FATHER
I'm sensing a little hostility.

DAUGHTER
You just won't let it go. You, Mom. "We're so proud of you." "You're going to be fine." Jesus.

FATHER
How evil.

DAUGHTER
Not…you know, if you say it once, it's meaningful. It's fine. But you both say it all the time. All the time. And the more you say it, the more it starts to sound a little…
"We're so proud of you"…so don't disappoint us.
"You're going to be fine"…as long as you don't screw up.
And you guys say it all the time.
And then you bring me out here, tell your little story about the dire consequences of one little screw-up…

(Makes crashing noise.)

Not exactly subtle, you know?

FATHER
I was talking about Navy Pier.

DAUGHTER
I swear to God, Roger is the only sane one of all of you.

Ohio & The Lake: Navy Pier

FATHER
You're not his daughter.

DAUGHTER
That's right.

FATHER
You're not his only child.

DAUGHTER
I'm not *your* only child.

(Long pause.)

I mean, it's not like this is a new thing. Not like you say it all the time, but…it's always there. Make good grades, make good choices, make us proud, make up for…
I mean, I know I'm the replacement, right, and the replacement, no matter how good they are, you're always thinking about the original, and maybe the replacement just can't ever be as good as the original, and so you're always waiting for the screw-up. And so you keep reminding them.

FATHER
Reminding?

DAUGHTER
Not…just…I know, OK. I'm the replacement, so I'd better not screw it all up.

(Silence.)

You know, this would be the time to say "Oh no, honey, you're not the replacement."

(Pause.)

FATHER
Yeah, well…maybe you should have this conversation with your mother, then.

(*A moment, then she stands and starts off.*)

Come back here.

DAUGHTER
I don't want to—

FATHER
You don't just drop something like that, that "replacement" stuff on someone and walk away. That's childish. You want to be treated like an adult? Start acting like one.

(*Beat.*)

Sit down.

(*Pause. She sits.*)

You forget, you know? You live in America, and you forget...you never even think about...
You do everything you're supposed to. Go to the doctor. Lamaze classes. Check everything off the list. And it's all supposed to be fine.

(*Beat.*)

It all happens really fast, when it happens. So fast, that no one has time to answer a question. All these people, rushing in, rushing around, rushing her out. Surgery. And I was in the waiting room. Alone.
And, you know, you pray. For both of them, of course, for both of them to be OK. At first. And then there's this voice...back of your head. Voice of the devil. "Choose." If you can only have one of them make it. And that voice, it gets louder, and it won't shut up until, finally, you do.
You choose your wife.

DAUGHTER
Because you can always have another baby.

FATHER

Yeah.
And I know that if your mom had to make the choice, she would have chosen the baby. Because…I don't know. I think any mom would.
But…when they finally came out and told me what had…that she was OK, but the baby…I was…grateful. Yeah.
And she was devastated, you know, of course. And I was sad, too, yeah, I mean, torn up, you know? But still…grateful. So it wasn't as bad. For me. Except, you know, seeing her, so…and not being able to help.
So one day you think, maybe we should see if we can try again.

DAUGHTER

For a replacement.

FATHER

Yeah.

DAUGHTER

Wow.
OK, that's…wow. I mean, I always knew you thought it, but I never thought you'd ever actually say it.
OK, then, we should just—

FATHER

Sit down.

DAUGHTER

No, no we should really—

FATHER

No, sit down, just…
Come on. Sit down. Please. Please.
I'm not finished.

DAUGHTER

Oh, I can hardly wait to hear the rest of this.

FATHER
Yeah, well, this was not on my list of things to talk about today.

DAUGHTER
I mean, all the stuff about how she was on total bed rest, and the Caesarean, and all the—

FATHER
Think you know everything.

DAUGHTER
I knew this.

FATHER
I'm not done.
Come on. Please, just…

DAUGHTER
OK, fine.

FATHER
All right. So you know all about the difficult pregnancy. Sure. But the thing is—and this is the thing you can't know—is when they hand you this little human being, you know that all those things you were afraid of up until then, those things are over. And all the…unknown stuff, the stuff you can't foresee, it's still waiting for you.
And it…you do not know what it is like to be afraid until you are afraid for somebody else. Before, I was afraid for your mother. But right then, I was afraid for you.
And that's when you stopped being the replacement baby. Since then, you've always been just "the baby."

DAUGHTER
Always "the baby."

FATHER
Jesus, are you going to nail me on every word I say?

DAUGHTER
So, you're still afraid I'm going to screw up.

FATHER
Yes.

DAUGHTER
What do I have to do to prove I'm not a screw-up?

FATHER
You're not a screw-up. I'm not a screw-up. But I screw up.
Everyone screws up. Everyone.
Planes in the lake.
Just because I worry, it doesn't mean I think you're a screw-up. It's just…you're like everyone else, OK? Like me.
There was a time, you know…I thought I did it. That choice I made, I thought—a little—that I somehow made it happen.

DAUGHTER
Wow. Ego much?

FATHER
Parental prerogative.
So yeah, I was grateful and guilty and just a little bit mental. Like this is a shock to you.
Scared. They hand you a person, and you know that you have an infinite capacity for doing harm to that person. And you have this…this…fear. That even if you do everything right, and check everything off the list, that something will happen. Fast. And there won't be anything to do about it.
And, you know, it hasn't really gone according to plan up to now.
Your mom and me.
It's not easy.

(Pause.)

DAUGHTER
You ever think about him?

FATHER
Yeah. I do.

DAUGHTER
Me, too.

FATHER
I gather.

DAUGHTER
I used to make up all these dumb-ass little stories about him, my big brother, little kid stuff, stupid stuff really. Doesn't matter. Right now, though, I just…wish I had someone to go first. So I could watch. And so you and Mom wouldn't be so mental about me. But basically so I could watch him and see what to do, what not to… So I wouldn't have to…

FATHER
Yeah.

DAUGHTER
Watch and learn, you know?

FATHER
Good system.

DAUGHTER
But I don't have anyone to go first.

FATHER
Doesn't always help. I had your Uncle Mike, and he really wasn't…

DAUGHTER
Yeah, well, that's Uncle Mike.

(They laugh. It's brittle.)

My big brother would *not* have been like Uncle Mike.

FATHER

No. No, he wouldn't.

(They sit in silence.)

DAUGHTER

Philadelphia's far.

FATHER

Yeah.

(She leans against him. He puts his arm around her. They sit. The sound of a jet overhead, eastbound. End of play.)

Division & California:
Steel Flags

By Yolanda Nieves

Copyright 2011 by Yolanda Nieves. All rights reserved. CAUTION: Professionals and amateurs are hereby warned that *Division & California: Steel Flags* is subject to a royalty. They are fully protected by the copyright laws of the United States of America and of all countries covered by the international Copyright Union (included the Dominion of Canada and the rest of the British Commonwealth), the Berne Convention, the Pan-American Copyright Convention and the University Copyright Convention, as well as all rights, including professional and amateur stage rights, motion picture, recitation, lecturing, public reading, radio broadcasting, television, video or sound recording, all other forms of mechanical or electronic reproduction, such as CD-ROM, CD-I, DVD, information storage and retrieval systems and photocopying, and the rights of translation into foreign languages, are strictly reserved. Particular emphasis is laid upon the matter of readings, permission for which must be secured in writing.

Required royalties must be paid every time this play is performed before any audience, whether or not it is presented for profit and whether or not admission is charged. To obtain stock and amateur performance rights, you must contact:

Yolanda Nieves
yolnieves@sbcglobal.net

Playwright Biography

Yolanda Nieves was born and raised in Chicago's Humboldt Park neighborhood, and is a poet, playwright, director, educator, actress, and creative director of The Vida Bella Ensemble. She has been featured on Vocalo, WGN TV News, and NPR, and her play, *The Brown Girls' Chronicles* has been nationally acclaimed. As an educator, Ms. Nieves is committed to using the oral tradition on stage as a way to create consciousness of how the past influences who we are becoming as a community. Currently, she is an assistant professor, is working on a new collection of stories and plays, and still lives in Humboldt Park.

Acknowledgments

Division & California: Steel Flags premiered as part of The Chicago Landmark Project in June 2011. It was directed by Ed Cisneros with the following cast:

COOKIE	Marcel Asilis
LA MATADORA (SONIA)	Damariz Posadas
MOTHER	Jasmin Cardenas
GRANDMOTHER	Carmen Cenko

Division & California: Steel Flags

Cast
COOKIE, an eleven year old girl
LA MATADORA (SONIA), Cookie's older sister, twelve years old
MOTHER, in her early thirties
GRANDMOTHER, in her early fifties

Setting
An apartment building on the corners of Division Street and California Avenue in Chicago. A tiny kitchen stage left, Sonia and Cookie's crowded bedroom stage right.

Time
The present.

Division & California: Steel Flags

Damariz Posadas in *Division & California: Steel Flags*

The Chicago Landmark Project
June – July, 2011
Produced by Theatre Seven of Chicago
Photo by Amanda Clifford

Division & California: Steel Flags
by Yolanda Nieves

(It is late evening. Two little girls, Sonia and Cookie, are on stage. They are jumping rope, or playing hopscotch, reciting a playground chant by the light of the full moon that reflects the shadow of a steel Puerto Rican flag.)

COOKIE and SONIA

Papi's gone,
and Mami cries
my sister's mad
and so am I.

Where is Papi?
High, jail, dead.
High, jail, dead.
High, jail, dead.

(Lights on Cookie.)

(Sonia takes out a red cloth and starts waving the cloth as if she were fighting a bull on stage.)

COOKIE
Drunk on my uncle's leftover can of beer that we shared, my sister decided that she was going to go by the name of La Matadora. La Matadora Sonia Felipa Gonzalez. From Humboldt Park, Division Street and California Avenue! She wasn't going to take it anymore. That's what she declared under the steel Puerto Rican flag that salutes the park.

SONIA
(Proudly, to no one in particular.) I am La Matadora! There's no reason why I can't be a bull-fighting woman just like those boys in the Spanish films.

(She takes a cigarette and puts it in her mouth. She keeps swinging the cape.)

(Lights out on Sonia. Meanwhile Mother and Grandmother pass out "Have You Seen This Girl?" flyers amongst the audience.)

COOKIE
It's been over a week since my sister disappeared. A week since she turned twelve and a half. Eye-witnesses came forward like an explosion. First they said it was a white man in a white van, with no windows. Two days later they said it is was a Puerto Rican man in a black mustang with tinted windows. I couldn't believe the neighbors' gossip. For a couple of days, I hoped my sister's picture would be all over the news. But no one was interested in some lost Puerto Rican kid - especially a girl from Division and California. Some of our family drove in from Indiana. We held hands together, cried on each others' shoulders, and passed out homemade flyers all over Humboldt Park, begging anyone to tell us if my sister was dead or alive.

(Lights up on Mother and Grandmother sitting at kitchen table.)

MOTHER
(Hysterically) Her father's to blame. I don't know if he's high, in jail, or dead! What an example he was!

GRANDMOTHER
Dios sabe todas las cosas. Don't worry. We'll find her.

MOTHER
If he had been a real man, like the ones on T.V., and paid more attention to his daughters then this wouldn't have happened. I knew he had other women. Pero se lo soporte…I accepted it. Then he just got up and left. Sonia has followed in his footsteps. Why me?

(Lays her head in her arm and quietly weeps.)

COOKIE
(Sadly) My grandmother nodded, and stroked the curve of my mother's weeping back.

MOTHER

Some nights, when I can't sleep, I stare out the window, at the steel flag, and feel my heart grow stiff like its metal. When the orange eye of the sun burns through the hollow star, I fix the coffee, but I burn with the poison of knowing that my husband is being dishonest with me with other women. Dios me perdone, but I am starting to hate him.

He farts in his sleep, talks with his mouth full of rice and beans, and leaves his shaving cream to crust hard on the bathroom mirror.

But all I think about is my girls who have this good-for-nothing as a father. And I pray they don't hate me like I used to hate my mother for staying in marriage from hell.

(Grandmother sees Cookie watching and walks toward her.)

GRANDMOTHER

Ju…come here!

(Takes off her slipper and throws it at Cookie. They run around the kitchen table a bit.)

COOKIE

(To audience) Oh, no! That old woman has eyes as sharp as spikes! She knows!

(Cookie runs off to the other side of the stage and Grandmother, who has one hand on her hips and the other holding the other slipper, is nodding knowingly. They Freeze. Lights down on Mother. Mother and Grandmother exit. Enter Sonia. Lights up on Sonia.)

SONIA

He's not any taller than me. He has these little red pimples outlining the frame of his jaw, but he loves bullfighting, because he said, his uncles had a bull on a ranch in Texas. Saturno Rodriguez Boyas Zapata! He's only a year older than me, but is the boy I have been waiting for my whole life. He slow-circled me right under the steel flag. My heart waved when he promised me a future with the bull, away from the crowded slouchy bed we have to share with my two fat younger cousins, and away from our squeezed up apartment where no one can breathe and everyone has to huddle in close when they walk.

(Changing her voice to Saturno's): Orale. Ven conmigo. Together we will conquer the world and kills some bulls!

(Sonia takes the cape out and starts to swing it pretending to fight a bull. Sonia then wraps her cape around her hips and moves toward Cookie. Lights up on Cookie and Sonia. There is a picture of a full moon projected on the back of stage.)

COOKIE
(To audience - both Cookie and Sonia pantomiming the actions.) The night of the full moon, before she escaped, she woke me up, and we climbed out of the window, tiptoed across the porch, and poured ourselves on the cold gray porch stairs.

SONIA
I'm leavin'.

COOKIE
No shit! Where to?

SONIA
Swear to God and on our father's grave! Then I'll tell ya.

COOKIE
Is Papi dead?

SONIA
Who cares? He doesn't. This isn't about him. This is about me! Got two bus tickets to Texas. There's bullfighting in Texas, and Saturno's been saving up his birthday money. It's like the dream I dreamed!

COOKIE
Are you gonna get married?

SONIA

Married? *(Laughs out loud.)* You really are a pendeja! Ain't never gonna get married. Ain't gonna do what Mom did. I gotta live the life I want…. I'm going to fight bulls! We're meeting under the flag tonight!

(Lights out on Sonia. Exit Sonia. Lights up on Grandmother.)

GRANDMOTHER

Sonia running away…e-it's his fault. Pretty soon theeze girls will want to e-stand next to cars that park under the flag and thump like earthquakes…BOOM-PA-PA-BOOMP-PA-PA-BOOMP. That music makes me feel like my heart is throbbing outside my chest on a chain! And then they will es-swagger with boys into alleys. It's not e-supposed to be like that, but that is wah happens when girls don't have a padre.

My daughter's husband…I want to say he was a tecato-loser. I want to say he had too much gold around his neck for a man. But in the beginning he was not that bad. I liked him - he was like my son.

Then one day I find the cell phone ringing. On the line a woman said she was going to dar a luz - have the loser's baby.

I said nothing to nobody, but I cried into a pañuelo because I was sooo mad! Then I did what I had to do. I told him to choose between my daughter or that puta.

So…se fue - he left - ran like a drunk chicken who knew heez neck was gonna be twisted and cracked for dinner. Mejor! Better for everybody! But I feel it-right here! *(Points to her heart.)*

COOKIE

At the end of the week, when the news went on about some other missing neighborhood girl, and friends and relatives folded back to their normal lives, my abuela cornered me in our tiny sweaty bathroom.

(Cookie now has a toothbrush in her hand and looks into the audience - the audience is a pretend mirror.)

GRANDMOTHER
Where is she? Tu sabes, don't you? Ju know esomsing...

COOKIE
(To Grandmother.) Where's who? ¿Quien? *(To audience.)* I didn't like the way I sounded to myself. There's a hole inside me now-as big as that one star on the flag that stares at me through the window. The hole is getting bigger every day. If I tell my Grandmother where she is, Sonia will hate me forever. *(Cookie walks back to Grandmother.)* If I don't tell I might never see her again.

GRANDMOTHER
(Grabbing Cookie by the hair.) It's in jour face...Tell me or eso help jou...Si no me dices te voy a romper los dientes - and I will make esure those pretty little teeth don't grow back.

COOKIE
(To Grandmother.) Ouch! All right, Abuela, all right! *(To the audience.)* I was forced to spit the whole story out along with my toothpaste. But I got to keep my teeth.

(Lights up on Sonia.)

SONIA
Traitor! Dream-killer! *(Sonia still has the cape and whirls it around.)* Why did she have to tell? Everybody wants me to be sorry, but I'm not sorry. Next time, I won't tell anybody. I'll keep my secrets to myself. Next time, I'll have a better plan, and then who'll be sorry? The rest of the world! That's who!

(Lights out on Sonia. Exit Sonia.)

COOKIE
Traitor. Dream-killer. That's what my sister calls me now. What do I care that La Matadora came back exhausted, hungry, and disappointed? And that the Texas police and the Chicago police scolded her, our mother, Saturno and his mother for being - how

do you say it? Burros and sanganos. Still, I'm a little jealous. I wonder if La Matadora ever even got to fight a bull. For now I have to stick with the boring and ordinary. With going shopping at the tiendita with my mother. With taking care of my two fat cousins who think they can swim in the Humboldt Park lagoon, but will only drown. I'm hoping La Matadora will forgive me. Hell, in a week or two, I'll sneak a beer from my uncle's stash, steal a cigarette from my mother's purse, and ask La Matadora myself. Cross my heart. I'll do it.

(Cookie jumps rope alone. The stage darkens as the full moon rises. The audience sees the shadow of the steel Puerto Rican flag.)

Papi's gone
and Mami cries,
my sister's mad,
and so am I!

(Lights out. End play.)

Logan & Milwaukee: Logan Square Farmers Market

By Laura Jacqmin

Music by Andy Lutz
Lyrics by Laura Jacqmin

Copyright 2011 by Laura Jacqmin. All rights reserved. CAUTION: Professionals and amateurs are hereby warned that *Logan & Milwaukee: Logan Square Farmers Market* is subject to a royalty. They are fully protected by the copyright laws of the United States of America and of all countries covered by the international Copyright Union (included the Dominion of Canada and the rest of the British Commonwealth), the Berne Convention, the Pan-American Copyright Convention and the University Copyright Convention, as well as all rights, including professional and amateur stage rights, motion picture, recitation, lecturing, public reading, radio broadcasting, television, video or sound recording, all other forms of mechanical or electronic reproduction, such as CD-ROM, CD-I, DVD, information storage and retrieval systems and photocopying, and the rights of translation into foreign languages, are strictly reserved. Particular emphasis is laid upon the matter of readings, permission for which must be secured in writing.

Required royalties must be paid every time this play is performed before any audience, whether or not it is presented for profit and whether or not admission is charged. To obtain stock and amateur performance rights, you must contact:

>Laura Jacqmin
>c/o Derek Zasky
>William Morris Endeavor Entertainment
>1325 Avenue of the Americas
>New York, NY 10019

Playwright Biography

Laura Jacqmin was the winner of the 2008 Wasserstein Prize, a $25,000 award to recognize an emerging female playwright. Her play *Ski Dubai* was produced in Steppenwolf Theatre Company's 5th Annual First Look Repertory of New Work; her play *Look, We Are Breathing* was workshopped at the 2010 Sundance Theatre Lab on Governors Island, directed by Mark Brokaw. Other plays include *Folk Song, Dental Society Midwinter Meeting, Do-Gooder* and *And We Awoke There Was Light Was Light*. Her work has been produced and developed by the Goodman Theatre, Ars Nova, Joe's Pub, Second Stage, Ensemble Studio Theatre, Victory Gardens Theater, Chicago Dramatists, The 24 Hour Plays Off-Broadway, the Contemporary American Theatre Festival and more. From 2007 to 2008, she was a contributing writer for *The Onion A.V. Club* and *A.V. Club Chicago*. Jacqmin is a member of the 2010-2011 playwrights unit at the Goodman Theatre. She lives in Chicago where she is currently working on commissions from the Goodman Theatre, InterAct Theatre and Ensemble Studio Theatre. BA Yale University; MFA Ohio University.

Acknowledgments

Logan & Milwaukee: Logan Square Farmers Market premiered as part of The Chicago Landmark Project in June 2011. It was directed by Richard Perez with the following cast:

LIZZIE	Victoria Blade
MILTON	Greg Williams

Logan & Milwaukee: Logan Square Farmers Market

Cast
LIZZIE, late 20s or 30s. Must actually be able to play the guitar (well). She's wearing a dress – the kind that pretty girls wear in the summer time.
MILTON, late 20s or 30s. African-American. Must be able to play the triangle passably well. Or poorly. Really, either would work. He's wearing a button-down shirt and trousers – he looks like he might be going to work.

Setting
The Logan Square Farmers Market. A Sunday.

Time
Probably right around 10am.

Greg Williams and Victoria Blade in *Logan & Milwaukee: Logan Square Farmers Market*

The Chicago Landmark Project
June – July, 2011
Produced by Theatre Seven of Chicago
Photo by Amanda Clifford

Logan & Milwaukee: Logan Square Farmers Market
by Laura Jacqmin
Music by Andy Lutz
Lyrics by Laura Jacqmin

(Lizzie is here. She has a guitar case open by her feet. It contains several lonely dollar bills.)

(Lizzie is strumming the guitar, which is probably why the case is relatively empty – if you get my meaning. But let me clarify: she's good at the guitar. She's just a terrible lyricist.)

LIZZIE
(Singing:)

THEY SELL 27 VARIETIES OF SQUASH
IN THAT CORNER
BY THE HYDRANT

THEY SELL 3 VARIETIES OF ONIONS
IN THAT CORNER
BY THE HYDRANT

YELLOW, GREEN, AND RED
ANOTHER NAME FOR THE GREEN ONES
IS
SCALLIONS

(She strums for a moment; maybe inspiration will come? It's not, so: the same thing, but different words)

THEY SELL 9 DIFFERENT VARIETIES OF GREENS
IN THAT CORNER
BY THE DOG
OH WAIT THE DOG IS GONE
THE DOG IS BACK
A DIFFERENT DOG IS ALSO THERE NOW

THEY SELL KALE, LETTUCE, SPINACH, TURNIP
GREENS, MACHE, FRISEE, ENDIVE, MICROGREENS
AND CHARD
IN THAT CORNER
BY THE DOGS.

(She stops playing the guitar. She speaks to an unseen crowd of people.)

Good morning!
I'm Lizzie.
You may recognize me from a two-song set I played at the Empty Bottle in Fall of 2008 during the holiday craft fair.
You may also recognize me from last year's farmers markets in Andersonville, and Hyde Park, and Lincoln Square, and Lincoln Park, and Bronzeville, and –
They decided to go in a different direction. But it's no big deal.
Because Logan Square is my home and Logan Square is my artistic muse, so thank you for supporting Logan Square artists at the Logan Square Farmers Market!
Financial support is appreciated, as is – um – applause.

(Beat. No applause is forthcoming.)

So – this being the official opening day of the market – and it being exactly 10:01 a.m., exactly one minute after the official opening time, I would like to officially announce that I am now the official Logan Square Farmers Market artist in residence.
Musician in residence.
Artist in residence.
Both!
Officially.
As of today.
Dibs.
If you'd like to hear a song, just please drop some change in the guitar case.

(Suddenly, Milton enters with another, medium-to-large-sized instrument case. It should be a fairly mysterious instrument case. What, exactly, might be inside of this instrument case? Lizzie eyes him suspiciously. He doesn't eye her at all – just gets set up without taking a second glance at her.)

(Is he? He might be. Is he? He totally is. He's going to busk, right here, right now. That son of a bitch.)

MILTON

Good afternoon, ladies and gentlemen.
It's a beautiful Sunday in June, isn't it? It's just so goddamn beautiful. There are birds. There is grass. It is 71 goddamn degrees in Chicago, and you know what I love to do when the weather is this fine?
You know what I <u>have</u> to do?
I have to sing.

LIZZIE

Um, excuse me!
Excuse me!
Hello!

MILTON

Good morning!

LIZZIE

You can't do that.
You can't busk here.

MILTON

I was just going to play a song.

LIZZIE

For free?

MILTON

Well – I'm accepting donations.

LIZZIE

Right. You're busking.

MILTON

Okay: I'm busking.

LIZZIE
But – I don't think you understand.
This is my corner.
This is the best corner.
Everyone has to pass this corner to go between the first section of the market and the second section of the market.
If you came here for organic gelato, you gotta go to my left.
If you came here for a grass-fed beef burger, you gotta go to my right.
And if you realize you want organic gelato after you eat your grass-fed beef burger, you have to pass me twice.
This is kind of the perfect spot. And it's kind of mine.

MILTON
Free country.

LIZZIE
Excuse me?

MILTON
Free country.
If you can play a song, I can play a song.

LIZZIE
Wrong.

MILTON
Wrong?

LIZZIE
Wrong.
I mean, it's not just this corner. It's not just the principle of the thing, okay?
You're talking to the official Logan Square Farmers Market artist in residence.

MILTON
Musician in residence?

LIZZIE

Both!
Officially.

MILTON

You want to see something?

LIZZIE

Depends on the something.

(Milton raises his t-shirt, showing her something.)

Ew! What is that?

MILTON

That's a very good question! And I don't know the answer to it.
And I need twenty bucks to go to the Target walk-in clinic so a non-health-insurance-requiring doctor can tell me what it is.

LIZZIE

Look: I feel for you, but this is my turf.
What do you think would happen if I just let any guy with a weird growth on his stomach bump me out of my spot?
I called dibs. My dibs stands.

MILTON

You dibs-ed this whole lawn thing here? This whole entire lawn thing, with all the impromptu yard sales, and the picnics, and the kid with the sign who gives back rubs for thirty cents?

LIZZIE

That kid creeps me out.

MILTON

He's only like ten.

LIZZIE

Where are his parents?

MILTON
I mean, it <u>seems</u> harmless –

LIZZIE
But you never know.

MILTON
That's what I say!

LIZZIE
That's what I say, too!

(They smile. Beat.)

I mean –
That's what I <u>said</u>.
That's what I've <u>been</u> <u>saying</u>.
That's what I said <u>first</u>!

MILTON
Look, I'm sorry? But this is happening.

LIZZIE
Man. You don't even know, do you? You don't even <u>know</u> what the music scene at this farmers market used to be like.
There was a time?
When there were kids?
And those kids would bring, like, a <u>boombox</u>?
And those kids would play the boombox?
And they would just – dance. Sort of – half-heartedly.
Just dance.
And they were like, pay us for doing this.
Ri<u>dic</u>ulous.
Things were very, very different before I came along.
I've struggled long and hard.
I've paid so many tickets, I can't even count the number of times I've had to go downtown to the courthouse – with my guitar! – to state my case in front of a judge.
I have paid my dues – literally – and now this farmers market <u>will</u> have a quality music scene that everyone can take seriously! Or else!

(Over the course of this, Lizzie has lost track of Milton a little and has stopped watching him. So when she turns back to him, she sees that now he's set up his busking station.

Oh, and by the way: he plays the triangle)

LIZZIE
You have got to be kidding me.

MILTON
'Fraid I'm not.
I'm gonna rock this farmers market, like it or not.
There are a lot of white people with dogs roaming around in this general vicinity who are totally gonna dig what I've got to offer.

LIZZIE
So play your song then.

MILTON
I think I will.

(Milton prepares. He dangles the triangle. He prepares the beater. He begins his song.)

WHAT IS THE DIFFERENCE
BETWEEN A PICKLE AND A CUCUMBER?

THIS IS ACTUALLY A TRICK QUESTION
THERE ISN'T ONE

(Beat. Milton puts down the triangle and the beater.)

That is just one of many. One of many, many more.

(Lizzie is dumbstruck.)

Nothing to say to that, huh? Don't you have some response you'd like to fling my way? Are you gonna try to take my clanger next?

'Cause if you try to take my clanger, I'll clang you with it – I have no problem clanging you.

LIZZIE

That was –

MILTON

All right, here we go.

LIZZIE

That was –

MILTON

Lay it on me!

LIZZIE

That was <u>awesome</u>.
I mean . . .
I try to do the same thing sometimes? To integrate my surroundings into my songs? But I've always found it very difficult to rhyme the word "organic" with anything.
Or baguette.
Or tomato.
Or crepe.

MILTON

Thank you.
<u>Thank</u> <u>you</u>.
Everyone told me it was stupid to play the triangle, you know? But I believed in the triangle, and I believed in <u>myself</u> and the triangle, and here we are, right?

LIZZIE

God, and I was so horrible to you.

MILTON

Naaah.

LIZZIE
And here you are, with this growth, and no health insurance, and all you need is twenty dollars –
That's, like, only an hour of busking!
If you're good. I mean. If you're good, I hear you can make that much in an hour.

MILTON
How much have you made?

LIZZIE
I mean, the farmer's market just opened, so . . .

MILTON
You've got a few dollars in there, though.

LIZZIE
I put those in. They're seed dollars. To get the ball rolling.

MILTON
Oh.

LIZZIE
Shit.
Who am I kidding?
The most I've <u>ever</u> made? At any of the farmers markets I've <u>ever</u> played at?
Has been six dollars. And I got the distinct feeling they were ironic dollars. Given for the sake of irony.
What if I can't even get any ironic dollars? <u>Here</u>? In Logan Square?

MILTON
Hey now.
Like you said: they just opened.
Maybe you just need – a better hook.
Like, maybe instead of a solo musician – you could be part of a duo.

LIZZIE
I don't know.

MILTON
One song?

(Beat.)

LIZZIE
One song.

(They begin playing.)

MILTON
PEOPLE SIT ON THAT GRASS
PEOPLE PLUNK DOWN THEIR ASS
ON THAT GREEN STRIP OF LAWN
WHERE YOUR PIT BULL HAS GONE

LIZZIE
AND BY GONE, HE MEANS POOP
EVACUATED BOWEL-BORN SOUP
I JUST WANTED A SQUASH
NOW MY SHOES NEED A WASH

MILTON
THIS IS A MARKET!

LIZZIE
NOT A DOG PARK!

MILTON
IF I WANTED DOGS I WOULD HAVE BROUGHT MY OWN
BUT

MILTON and LIZZIE
OH MY GOD YOUR DOG IS SO FREAKIN' CUTE (L)
BUT DON'T YOU GIVE A SHIT THAT HE'S A BIT OF A BRUTE? (M)

MILTON and LIZZIE *(cont.)*
HE JUST ATE MY WHOLE CROISSANT *(L)*
LICKED THAT HIPSTER CHICK'S BOUFFANT *(M)*
BUT OH MY FREAKIN' GOD YOUR DOG IS CUTE *(L and M)*

MILTON
IT'S JUST HIS FACE IS SO SWEET
ALL THE BABIES HE GREETS
COO AND GIGGLE AND GRIN
AS HE NOSES THEIR SHINS

LIZZIE
AND HIS OWNER'S SO HOT
LIKE IMPROBABLY HOT
HEY! DON'T YOU GIMME THAT SEXY SNEER
THEM'S THE RULES: THERE'S NO CRAP HERE!

MILTON
THIS IS IMPORTANT

LIZZIE
WE'RE NOT ASSHOLES

MILTON
IF YOUR DOG IS BAD, THEN YOU SHOULD JUST STAY HOME
BUT

LIZZIE and MILTON
OH MY GOD YOUR DOG IS SO FREAKIN' CUTE *(L and M)*
BUT DON'T YOU GIVE A SHIT THAT HE'S A BIT OF A BRUTE? *(L and M)*
HE JUST BIT THAT BASSET HOUND *(M)*
MY CREPE SUZETTE, HE STOLE AND DOWNED *(L)*

LIZZIE AND MILTON *(cont.)*
BUT OH MY FREAKIN' GOD YOUR DOG IS CUTE *(L and M)*

(She beats on the guitar for a few beats. Then, for the finale, perhaps just a chord or two and:)

OH MY FREAKIN' GOD YOUR DOG IS CUTE *(L and M)*

(They smile at each other. Is there any more money in the case? Nah – but they've got all day. End of play.)

63rd & Woodlawn: Robust Coffee Lounge

By Brian Golden

Copyright 2011 by Brian Golden. All rights reserved. CAUTION: Professionals and amateurs are hereby warned that *63rd & Woodlawn: Robust Coffee Lounge* is subject to a royalty. They are fully protected by the copyright laws of the United States of America and of all countries covered by the international Copyright Union (included the Dominion of Canada and the rest of the British Commonwealth), the Berne Convention, the Pan-American Copyright Convention and the University Copyright Convention, as well as all rights, including professional and amateur stage rights, motion picture, recitation, lecturing, public reading, radio broadcasting, television, video or sound recording, all other forms of mechanical or electronic reproduction, such as CD-ROM, CD-I, DVD, information storage and retrieval systems and photocopying, and the rights of translation into foreign languages, are strictly reserved. Particular emphasis is laid upon the matter of readings, permission for which must be secured in writing.

Required royalties must be paid every time this play is performed before any audience, whether or not it is presented for profit and whether or not admission is charged. To obtain stock and amateur performance rights, you must contact:

>   Brian Golden
>   Artistic Director, Theatre Seven of Chicago
>   1341 W Fullerton Ave
>   Suite 325
>   Chicago, IL 60614

Playwright Biography

Brian Golden is the Managing Artistic Director and a founding member of Theatre Seven of Chicago. During his time as Artistic Director, Theatre Seven's work has been seen by 8,000 patrons and the company has been nominated for one Jeff Award, two Black Theatre Alliance Awards, been named a finalist for Broadway in Chicago's Emerging Theatre Award and employed over 160 artists. For Theatre Seven, Brian has directed *The Water Engine: An American Fable*, *Hunting and Gathering*, *Diversey Harbor*, *The Sand Castle*, *Killing Women* and *Is Chicago*, and his play *Cooperstown* was nominated for a Joseph Jefferson Award. Brian is a graduate of Washington University in St. Louis, a two-time winner of the A.E. Hotchner Playwriting Contest, and recipient of the Leota Diesel Ashton Playwriting Prize and John J. Jutkowitz Award. He is an Executive Director Mentor as part of the League of Chicago Theatres' Mentorship Program, and serves as a Neighborhood Leader in the League's new ThinkTank.

Acknowledgments

63rd & Woodlawn: Robust Coffee Lounge premiered as part of The Chicago Landmark Project in June 2011. It was directed by Rebekah Scallet with the following cast:

JANEY	Katie Genualdi
BRUCK	George Zerante
AARON	Kroydell Galima
FOSTER	Ryan Hallahan

63rd & Woodlawn: Robust Coffee Lounge

Cast
JANEY, mid 20s: an elementary school teacher
BRUCK, late 20s: a PhD candidate in history
AARON, late 20s: a graduate student in history
FOSTER, early 20s: an undergraduate

Setting
Robust Coffee Lounge, at the intersection of 63rd Street & Woodlawn Avenue, Chicago.

Time
A warm day at the beginning of summer.

Katie Genualdi, George Zerante, Kroydell Galima and Ryan Hallahan in *63rd & Woodlawn: Robust Coffee Lounge*

The Chicago Landmark Project
June – July, 2011
Produced by Theatre Seven of Chicago
Photo by Amanda Clifford

63rd & Woodlawn: Robust Coffee Lounge
by Brian Golden

(Robust Coffee Lounge. Bruck and Janey hold hands and stand close to one another in front of the pastry display. They lean over it to look closer.)

JANEY

The one with the swirl.

BRUCK

You're going to regret that.

JANEY

It looks so *yummy*.

BRUCK

You always say that with the chocolate ones. And you always regret it.

JANEY

Sometimes its worth it.

BRUCK

(Lightly). You're gonna regret it.

JANEY

Yeah? What's a little regret?

(They kiss on the mouth.)

And oh yeah. I'm *so predictable*. *Janey always gets the chocolate swirls then ends up with a stomach ache.* I'm not the only one you know? With. *Behavior.* Patterns.

BRUCK

Tell me.

JANEY

You know. *(Conspiratorially.)* Like how every time we have sex in the afternoon you take me out for coffee after 'cause you need a blueberry muffin.

(Bruck laughs. And shrugs.)

BRUCK
It makes me need a blueberry muffin.

(She stands and looks at him for a moment.)

JANEY
I am so glad I know you.

BRUCK
What?

JANEY
I'm just so glad I know you.

(Pause. He smiles.)

BRUCK
Aw shucks.

JANEY
I'm *serious*. It's just a compliment. Take. A compliment.

BRUCK
OK. I'm sorry. Thank you.

JANEY
There's just. It's a big world, you know? And. And. *Facebook*. Ugh. And like with the internet. And all the ways there are to *know who someone is*. We've all got access to like…you know, a hundred different, like, representations of someone's *identity*.

BRUCK
That's why I don't have Facebook.

JANEY
I know because that's different. That's different than *knowing someone*. This world my kids are growing up in, my God. I mean I

look around that classroom and I wonder if they'll ever really *know* a person in their whole lives. You know?

BRUCK
Yeah, I gotcha.

JANEY
You know? And like...in their school. Or in Chicago. There's *so many people*. And. You know? I don't even wanna know all of them. It's like the brain can only handle so many...

BRUCK
...a hundred and fifty...

JANEY
...meaningful relationships before it starts to, *yes you told me that*, before it starts to break down.

BRUCK
The ideal size of tribal communities through most of recorded history.

JANEY
Right. Oh, I love it that you know that. When we met though. At that *stupid* Halloween party. I just felt like. That's a guy I want in my one-fifty. That's a guy I could *know*.

BRUCK
You just liked my Superman costume.

JANEY
No. Hah. It wasn't. I mean...you liked my Joan Holloway costume too...

BRUCK
I sure did.

JANEY
I'm just trying to say I'm glad I know you. OK? OK, Mister?

(He nods. They kiss, and go back to looking at the pastry tray. Their backs are to the door. Through the door, Aaron and Foster walk in, holding hands. This is the cap to their awesome day.)

JANEY

I'm so glad you took me here. I knew it would be great because of how you talked about it. I don't even have to order, I could just look at these all day -

AARON

Excuse me, do you mind if we go ahead?

(Bruck and Janey turn around.)

JANEY

No, go ahead. We're not in a rush.

AARON

Bruck.

BRUCK

Aaron.

AARON

Hi.

(Awkward. What should they do? They should definitely shake hands. They shake hands.)

How are you?

BRUCK

I'm good. I'm good. How are *you*?

AARON

I'm good.

(Aaron makes a decision.)

This is Foster. My boyfriend.

(Foster shakes hands with Bruck, then Janey.)

BRUCK

Nice to meet you.

FOSTER

Pleasure. *(To Janey.)* Foster.

JANEY

Janey Witter.

BRUCK

Sorry. Sorry. This is Janey. My girlfriend Janey.

AARON

Oh. Hi.

(Aaron shakes Janey's hand.)

Aaron.

JANEY

You guys…

(Aaron waits for Bruck to field the question. He doesn't.)

AARON

The history department. Back. Few years ago. Bruck was a TA for my uh, a class I was taking my last year of undergrad.

JANEY

Oh. What class, Bruck?

BRUCK

I don't remember.

AARON

It was, uh. Tenorio. Yeah. History of…what was it?

BRUCK
History of...

AARON & BRUCK
History of Progressivism in the Americas.

JANEY
Wow.

AARON
That was it. That was the class. Bruck helped me get through that class. He really got me through it. We spent some late nights...

BRUCK
...studying for the uh...

AARON
...prepping for those legendary Tenorio exams.

BRUCK
Yeah.

AARON
You still in the department? Working through that PhD?

BRUCK
Yeah.

AARON
Your time must be about up, huh? You finishing this year? Wrapping up that dissertation?

BRUCK
Nah...I've got two more quarters to finish it actually. *(Aaron looks puzzled.)* I took some time off. Last fall.

AARON
Oh.

BRUCK

I took kind of a…sabbatical. Last fall. *(Pause.)* Just had some personal stuff that came up.

AARON

Oh, OK. Well, hope you got it taken care of.

BRUCK

I did, I did.

AARON

You're back at it now though?

(Bruck nods.)

JANEY

You're history, too?

AARON

No. No. I –

FOSTER

He moved on to something else.

AARON

I dropped out. And, uh, got lucky, and…

FOSTER

…yeah you did…

AARON

…and they had an open slot in the polisci masters program. So I ended up there.

JANEY

Oh. What happened to history? Bruck loves it, like, a crazy man.

> AARON
> I don't know, I. Flirted with it for a little while. But…it didn't work out. Got a fresh start over in polisci…I'm doing a little bit of research assistance for some of the ConGov graybeards.

> FOSTER
> You can just say Constitutional Government, you snob.

> AARON
> Sorry.

> FOSTER
> And don't be modest. It's not a little bit. He's spends fifty hours a week over there.

> JANEY
> Wow. Researching what?

> AARON
> Voting trends in post-colonial African Democracies.

> JANEY
> Wow. That is like. Way above my pay grade. I teach.

> AARON
> Oh cool. That's fantastic.

> JANEY
> Third grade. We don't get to post-colonialism until, like – god. Sometime between lockers and puberty.

> AARON
> It's not really that heady. It has a long name. It's not too bad.

> FOSTER
> He's glad he made the switch.

(Foster holds Aaron's hand.)

He's happier this way. History wasn't…

JANEY

Wasn't what?

FOSTER

Just wasn't a good fit. *(Pause.)* Too much to think about.

AARON

Oh like polisci research has no thinking. This coming from an *undergrad.*

(Foster laughs.)

BRUCK

So you're an undergrad, huh?

FOSTER

Yeah.

BRUCK

Sophomore? Junior?

FOSTER

Junior.

BRUCK

What do you study?

FOSTER

East Asian Philosophy. Emphasis on Confucian Thought.

BRUCK

I've heard that's really trendy.

FOSTER

Its *been* really trendy. For like. Twenty-five hundred years.

(Everybody laughs, especially Janey.)

BRUCK
You live on campus?

FOSTER
No.

BRUCK
It's a beautiful campus. Especially in fall. Some really good undergrad housing. Just built that kajillion dollar complex down on Ellis.

JANEY
Mmm hmm.

BRUCK
That place is really something.

FOSTER
It's alright.

BRUCK
You're lucky. I didn't do my undergrad here.

FOSTER
Where'd you do it?

BRUCK
Ah, you haven't heard of it.

AARON
Macalester. Wasn't it?

JANEY
Yeah, Macalester.

BRUCK
Its in the Twin Cities. Minnesota. You probably haven't heard of it. It's not a great school.

                    FOSTER
It's alright.

                    BRUCK
Well. *(Pause.)* You're lucky. Great program you're in. Great housing. Great, you know, just being here in the city…You know I never knew what the rush to move off-campus was. When you're nineteen. Cafeteria food and those dorm room laundry machines that cost like a dime. No electric bills. No *landlords*. I took it as long as I could get it. That was the life. Whydya wanna leave that all behind?

                    FOSTER
We live together.

                    BRUCK
Oh. *Alright*. Well. There ya go.

                    JANEY
That's *exciting*. How long have you two…

(Aaron and Foster look at each other.)

                    FOSTER
About a year…

                    AARON
Ten months.

                    FOSTER
OK, so *about a year* is pretty accurate.

                    AARON
Ten months. In the interest of historical accuracy. *(Slightly, to Bruck.)* Ten months.

(Bruck nods.)

JANEY
Well, I'm trying to talk him in to the big *shared living decision*, but…you know. The bachelor life dies hard.

AARON
Yeah. I know.

(Pause.)

FOSTER
Can you order for us? I'm dying for a cigarette.

(Aaron nods.)

AARON
Caramel latte?

FOSTER
And the biscotti.

AARON
Got it.

(Foster kisses Aaron. Foster turns out to Janey.)

FOSTER
So nice to meet you.

JANEY
And you as well.

(Foster extends a hand to Bruck.)

FOSTER
Nice to meet you finally.

(They shake.)

BRUCK
Nice to meet you.

(Foster exits, pulling out his cigarette. An uncomfortable pause.)

AARON
I should…

BRUCK
Go ahead.

(Aaron turns, steps up to the imaginary Robust employee.)

AARON
Two caramel lattes. One biscotti. And a blueberry muffin.

(Pause. He nods to the imaginary Robust employee: "Yes, I can wait a moment." He turns back to Bruck and Janey.)

So you guys enjoying this great weather?

BRUCK
Oh yeah. Great day for a walk down Cornell.

JANEY
So Progressivism was…what…a few years ago? Did you guys stay…you haven't been in touch since…Progressivism?

AARON
Yeah we stayed in touch. Bruck wrote me this killer recommendation for the history grad program, I was buying him Fin du Monde by the barrelful forever just to say thank you.

BRUCK
It's been awhile though.

AARON
How long's it been?

BRUCK
About a year. *(Pause.)* Haven't heard from this guy at all.

JANEY
Sounds like you've been real busy though.

AARON
Yeah, I have been.

BRUCK
And *happy*.

AARON
Yeah. I am. *(with a look out to Foster.)* We have similar tastes in coffee. And enlightenment thinkers.

BRUCK
Montesquieu?

AARON
Yeah.

JANEY
That too, huh? All you guys are just the same I guess...Well, one thing *you two* don't have in common is Bruck would never leave history. He loves the program. He's very happy. He's very happy, aren't you hon?

BRUCK
Yeah. I am.

JANEY
All these opportunities for important research. And the faculty, you know, from what it sounds like, is really supportive. They were so good to him after his sabbatical. That was when we met. He's always got some...new...eighteenth century...*feudal*...whatever to be reading about.

AARON
I bet.

JANEY
Happy as a clam. He wouldn't leave if you paid him.

(Janey reaches out to hold Bruck's hand.)

AARON

Oh, I understand. Believe me. *(Pause.)* History definitely, you know...has its charms. I still think about it sometimes.

BRUCK

Do ya?

AARON

I do. Some of our times back in Tenorio's Lair. *(Pause.)* I'll always love history. You know, from when I was a little kid. Reading texts of famous speeches, or, or like maps of the Pacific. The naval battles. Civil War battles. Assassinations. Things like that. I ate that stuff up.

JANEY

...you guys with the maps...

AARON

I've always loved that. But...you know, what I found. And. Was very disenchanting. The more I studied it, the more I got to know what history, or the study of it actually was...was that actually the study of history is...really...about studying lies.

JANEY

What do you mean?

BRUCK

It's not lies.

AARON

It is though.

BRUCK

Different perspectives maybe...

                    AARON
No its lies. 'Cause the study of history is really so much more about studying history-tellers than learning about actual events. Because whenever you're reading something, what you're really reading is...not *who won some battle*, but more...one person's attempt to define it. How they re-define the events of their life, or other people's lives in...a historical context. Often to create a new historical narrative, or reinforce a pre-existing one that they really want to be true. And you study enough history and you realize that historical narratives are always changing to fit the needs of people at different times. So...basically...I kind of gave up on history when I realized how much time I'd wasted watching the past constantly struggle to redefine itself. *(Pause.)* And once I realized *that*...I guess I needed to be in a field that...understood itself a little better. *(Pause.)* Sorry. Long answer to a short question.

(Ding, or something to indicate the coffees, biscotti and muffin are ready. Aaron grabs them from the imaginary Robust employee.)

Thanks. *(Pause.)* I should run. Really great running in to you guys. So nice to meet you.

(Janey smiles and nods.)

                    BRUCK
We should, uh...get together. You know. Catch up on Montesquieu.

                    AARON
Yeah. We should.

                    BRUCK
I just got these new cards.

(Bruck pulls out a business card.)

                    JANEY
I'm sure he still has your number.

(Aaron takes the card.)

                        BRUCK
Give me a call. We can…

                        AARON
Yeah…yeah. You know, I'm really swamped with the research, and…

                        JANEY
…you seem really busy…

                        AARON
…and like whatever free time I have I'm unpacking boxes at the new place. Trying to keep up with that guy. Where does the time go, you know?

                        JANEY
We know the feeling.

                        AARON
But yeah, you know. Give me a call. We'll see if we can find some time.

                        BRUCK
Alright.

                        AARON
Really lovely to meet you. Enjoy your muffins.

(Bruck nods. Janey smiles. Aaron exits. He walks out the door. They stand there a moment, quiet. Bruck looks at her, reaches out casually to hold her hand. She pulls her hand away, puts it on her purse strap. She gives him a questioning smile. End of play.)

Lincoln & Eastwood:
Laurie's Planet of Sound

By Brett Neveu

Copyright 2011 by Brett Neveu. All rights reserved. CAUTION: Professionals and amateurs are hereby warned that *Lincoln & Eastwood: Laurie's Planet of Sound* is subject to a royalty. They are fully protected by the copyright laws of the United States of America and of all countries covered by the international Copyright Union (included the Dominion of Canada and the rest of the British Commonwealth), the Berne Convention, the Pan-American Copyright Convention and the University Copyright Convention, as well as all rights, including professional and amateur stage rights, motion picture, recitation, lecturing, public reading, radio broadcasting, television, video or sound recording, all other forms of mechanical or electronic reproduction, such as CD-ROM, CD-I, DVD, information storage and retrieval systems and photocopying, and the rights of translation into foreign languages, are strictly reserved. Particular emphasis is laid upon the matter of readings, permission for which must be secured in writing.

Required royalties must be paid every time this play is performed before any audience, whether or not it is presented for profit and whether or not admission is charged. To obtain stock and amateur performance rights, you must contact:

Brett Neveu
brettneveu@gmail.com

Playwright Biography

Brett Neveu's recent productions include *Red Bud* with The Royal Court Theatre, *Odradek* with The House Theatre and *Do The Hustle* with Writers' Theatre. Recent past work includes productions with Writers' Theatre, The Goodman Theatre, The Royal Shakespeare Company, A Red Orchid Theatre, TimeLine Theatre Company and American Theatre Company. He is the recipient of the Ofner Prize for New Work, the Emerging Artist Award from The League of Chicago Theatres, an After Dark Award for Outstanding Musical (*Old Town* with Strawdog Theatre Company) and has developed plays with companies including The New Group, The Goodman Theatre, Steppenwolf Theatre, Victory Gardens and is a resident-alum with Chicago Dramatists. He is also an ensemble member of A Red Orchid Theatre, a member of The Playwrights' Union and a member of the Center Theatre Group's Playwrights' Workshop. Brett has been commissioned by The Royal Court Theatre, Manhattan Theatre Club, Steppenwolf Theatre Company, The Goodman Theatre, TimeLine Theatre Company, Writers' Theatre, Strawdog Theatre and has had several plays published through Broadway Play Publishing and Dramatic Publishing. Brett has taught writing at Northwestern University, DePaul University, Second City Training Center and currently lives in Los Angeles.

Acknowledgments

Lincoln & Eastwood: Laurie's Planet of Sound premiered as part of The Chicago Landmark Project in June 2011. It was directed by Eric Ziegenhagen with the following cast:

BRADFORD	Jonathan Baude
MONICA	Katy Albert

Cast
BRADFORD, 24
MONICA, 23

Setting
Laurie's Planet of Sound, Chicago. Near the vinyl "New Arrivals" bin.

Time
Deep winter. Present day.

Katy Albert and Jonathan Baude in *Lincoln & Eastwood: Laurie's Planet of Sound*

The Chicago Landmark Project
June – July, 2011
Produced by Theatre Seven of Chicago
Photo by Amanda Clifford

Lincoln & Eastwood: Laurie's Planet of Sound
by Brett Neveu

(The sound of The Jam's "Beat Surrender" begins (music by The Jam should continue until the song selection is changed as indicated in the script). Lights up on a set of mostly full vinyl record bins. The bins face upstage and labeling of "*NEW ARRIVALS*" also faces upstage. Bradford, a geek in a heavy winter coat, tall stocking cap (with hood over it), boots and fingerless gloves, carefully scans through the albums. Standing near Bradford is Monica. Monica is also bundled up, but she's gone for the more "thrift-store layer approach" with a nutty hat, colorful scarf and mittens. Monica watches Bradford look over the albums. A long pause as Monica becomes more agitated with each flip of a record.)

MONICA
Oh, uh --

(Bradford pauses, sensing Monica's presence, but does not turn to look at her. He resumes scanning over the albums.)

Eeh. Uh. Shit -- oh fuck, cool.

(Bradford pauses again. His face twists into a grumble. He returns to the albums.)

Fuck me. "The Payola$."

BRADFORD
Hm?

MONICA
"Hammer on a Drum." Fuck me.

BRADFORD
Mm-hm.

MONICA
What the shit, huh, am I right?

BRADFORD
Yeah...

MONICA
Oh god --

BRADFORD
Just --

MONICA
Sorry.

BRADFORD
No, it's --

MONICA
Yeah.

(Bradford scans the albums.)

Person who stands behind you and talks.

BRADFORD
Huh?

MONICA
Me. Person who blah blah blah fuck me cool shit fuck fuck blah blah, right?

BRADFORD
Mm.

MONICA
Sorry but, okay, but shit, okay -- "Hammer on a Drum," am I right? Fucking "Payola$." *(pause)* No fucking way.

(Bradford stops.)

"Age of" fucking "Plastic?"

(Bradford turns toward Monica. He stares at her for a moment. A pause.)

BRADFORD

"Age of Plastic." Buggles.

MONICA

Who got rid of "Age of Plastic" you think?

BRADFORD

Don't know.

MONICA

A saddie.

BRADFORD

A...?

MONICA

A saddie. A sad guy.

BRADFORD

Oh.

MONICA

Very sad, very sad indeed.

(A pause.)

BRADFORD

I like to think --

MONICA

What?

BRADFORD

I said I like to think some dude's mom cleaned out some dude's closet when he was out of town or got married and carted the shit out for a price, not knowing the dude was hanging onto the stuff for a reason.

MONICA
Yeah, here she is giving her kid's album collection the heave-ho and then he gets home and he's like "oh fuck!"

BRADFORD
Uh-huh.

MONICA
"Age of Plastic." "Clean Clean."

BRADFORD
Uh-huh. "Clean Clean."

MONICA
(singing) "Near ner near nee near near...Clean Clean."

BRADFORD
(sort of singing) "Pickin' up, Pickin' up the tee-eeeem."

MONICA
(robot singing) "Clean Clean."

(A pause. Bradford pulls his hood from off of his head. He fixes his hair. A pause.)

You gonna grab those?

BRADFORD
Grab which?

MONICA
The Payola$, the Buggles, the shit before, the early Bangles, the HŸsker DŸ?

BRADFORD
I was mostly just in from the cold.

MONICA
These dark days of Chicago.

BRADFORD
Dark days indeed. Like the hollow of my mind.

MONICA
The "hollow of your mind?"

BRADFORD
Sure. Or, you know, fucking cold as a fucking frozen dog shit. You know. Yeah.

(A pause. Monica laughs.)

MONICA
You live around here?

BRADFORD
Two blocks up that way.

MONICA
I'm in Andersonville.

BRADFORD
You hit the bins at The Brown Elephant?

MONICA
Yeah, but the clerks there, I think they're hip to the good stuff.

BRADFORD
You go looking and end up pawing through fourteen torn apart "Breakfast in Americas."

MONICA
Thirty scratched to hell Neil Diamond "Jazz Singers."

BRADFORD
Six or seven "Tapestrys."

MONICA
You mostly, what?

BRADFORD
Me? Mostly?

MONICA
(gesturing to the bins) Your thing mostly, what's your thing?

BRADFORD
Oh. I. Early eighties new wave mostly with a branch of mid-seventies glam and pure classic rock.

MONICA
Totally me too. Except for the pure classic.

BRADFORD
That's mostly a subset. Just a side project whim. Not my grail.

MONICA
I'm like that with K-Tel weirdness.

BRADFORD
Like that?

MONICA
My side project whim.

BRADFORD
"Goofy Greats," "Looney Tunes," "Dumb Ditties."

MONICA
I have all three of those albums!

BRADFORD
K-Tel is good stuff.

MONICA
But my main, too, is the low-ocho new wave.

BRADFORD
Any recents?

MONICA
Always looking for The Fems. And whatever. And what I saw in the bin right there.

BRADFORD
Oh, hey, you want me to skip back?

MONICA
Nah, keep flipping. I'm waiting for lightning strikes.

BRADFORD
Lightning.

MONICA
(with a weird french accent) You never know what treasures will surface...

(A beat. Bradford slowly flips the albums.)

BRADFORD
"Runaways."

MONICA
Got it.

BRADFORD
Good stuff.

MONICA
Um-hum.

(Continues to flip.)

Stop!

BRADFORD
Yeah. This. Yeah.

MONICA
You know that?

                        BRADFORD
Sure.

                        MONICA
Pull it.

(Bradford pulls the album. It's a copy of "Troublemakers", a compilation record put out by Warner Brothers in 1980.)

                        BRADFORD
"Troublemakers."

                        MONICA
What is that?

                        BRADFORD
It's a Warner Brothers double album promo from 1980 with cuts from Jonathan Richman, John Cale, Wire, Urban Verbs, and, uh, Pearl Harbor and the Explosions. Check it out.

(Bradford hands Monica the album. Monica's eyes go wide as she opens the double album.)

                        MONICA
Fucking Buggles! Fucking "Clean Clean!"

                        BRADFORD
Oh yeah I forgot.

                        MONICA
How weird is that that "Clean Clean" is on this fucking thing!

                        BRADFORD
Totally. True.

                        MONICA
What a crazy fucking coincidence!

BRADFORD
Yeah it is fucking crazy.

MONICA
We just sang it and what are the chances!

BRADFORD
The chances are small I bet.

MONICA
Fuck me! Small fucking chances! *(pauses as she looks over album)* Don't know Robin Lane --

BRADFORD
Robin Lane and the Chartbusters. Yep.

MONICA
"Social Fools?"

BRADFORD
Devo.

MONICA
Brian Briggs --

BRADFORD
Aw that's a great one. "Nervous Breakdown." Sort of a rockabilly --

MONICA
It's great?

BRADFORD
Yeah --

MONICA
Shit, okay, fuck me, hold on --

(Monica disappears with the album, exiting. A long pause as Bradford watches after her, then turns back to the new arrivals. Bradford distractedly picks through the albums before him. Suddenly, the store music goes silent and "Nervous Breakdown" plays over the store's speakers system. A pause. Bradford watches to see if Monica is coming. A long pause. Monica returns, album sleeve in hand.)

                      MONICA
Nice stuff!

                      BRADFORD
Yeah.

                      MONICA
Doo doo doo doooooo --

                      BRADFORD
(slightly bouncing to the beat) Uh-huh.

                      MONICA
You know Curtis?

                      BRADFORD
Curtis?

                      MONICA
Yeah.

                      BRADFORD
Yeah. Curtis.

                      MONICA
At the counter?

                      BRADFORD
Curtis. Yeah.

                      MONICA
He was just telling me the song's a cover of a --

BRADFORD
An Eddie Cochran song.

MONICA
Yeah. And --

BRADFORD
That it's classified as techno-rockabilly, I suppose, if you want to get specific.

MONICA
Right.

BRADFORD
Curtis read it from the liner notes.

MONICA
He what?

BRADFORD
Hand me the album.

(Monica hands Bradford the album.)

(reading) "The mysterious Brian Briggs is a performing newcomer whose revival of Eddie Cochran's memorable "Nervous Breakdown" successfully invents techno-rockabilly, and reaffirms the existence of black leather in upstate New York."

MONICA
Wow. Curtis sort of sucks.

BRADFORD
Never trust jerk-off record store clerks.

MONICA
Okay.

BRADFORD
Like Curtis.

                    MONICA
All right.

                    BRADFORD
I hear he's got Gonorrhea.

                    MONICA
Yeah?

                    BRADFORD
And bleeding mouth sores.

                    MONICA
Okay.

                    BRADFORD
And, like, a weird shaped ball sack.

                    MONICA
Okay then.

                    BRADFORD
A ball sack that's all shriveled like a whatever deflated balloon in the sun. At least that's the word on the street. All of that. About Curtis.

                    MONICA
Glad for the info.

                    BRADFORD
Sure. Anyhow. I'll go, uh, here -- have at the bin for a sec.

                    MONICA
Okay.

                    BRADFORD
Be right back.

(Bradford exits. Monica, her mirth growing, watches Bradford offstage. A short argument is heard between Curtis and Bradford that seems to involve the words "asshole" and "Curtis" and "creepy weirdo fuckface." The store suddenly goes quiet. The tones offstage then settle, and turn into words such as "sorry" and "didn't mean to yell at you" and "call you later, okay?" A pause. Bradford returns, album in hand.)

BRADFORD
Here, uh, hand me the album sleeve.

(Monica hands the sleeve to Bradford. Bradford returns the album to the sleeve.)

MONICA
Everything okay?

BRADFORD
Yeah. Maybe. Is it?

MONICA
Sure.

BRADFORD
Yeah?

MONICA
(smiling) Why not.

(A pause. Bradford holds the album out to Monica.)

BRADFORD
You should totally get this. It's great.

MONICA
Okay.

(Monica takes the album.)

BRADFORD
It's a great album. Not valuable. And kind of weird. And sort of rare. Mostly it's a good find. Something that you'll probably really enjoy a bunch of times over.

MONICA
A treasure.

BRADFORD
Maybe.

MONICA
Lightning.

BRADFORD
Lightning. Yeah.

(Monica holds up the album.)

MONICA
Lightning has struck.

(Haircut 100's "Love Plus One" begins to play.)

Haircut 100. Excellent.

BRADFORD
Yeah.

MONICA
Pure pop.

BRADFORD
With horns.

MONICA
Oh such funky stuff.

BRADFORD
But good funky stuff.

                    MONICA
Good funky stuff with clean-cut Brits in sweatervests.

                    BRADFORD
And awesomely rocking conga drums.

(Bradford and Monica listen for a moment.)

                    MONICA
You were here, yes?

(Monica points at the bins.)

                    BRADFORD
Yeah.

(Bradford moves back to the bins.)

                    MONICA
And I was here, yeah?

(Monica moves behind Bradford.)

                    BRADFORD
You were, yeah.

                    MONICA
Let's finish the stack and see what other treasure abounds.

                    BRADFORD
Okay.

                    MONICA
Okay.

(Bradford smiles at Monica. Monica smiles at Bradford. Bradford begins to flip through the albums until the chorus in the song plays.)

BRADFORD
(sort of singing) "Ring and a ring and a ring and a ring."

MONICA
(singing) "Love, love, love plus one."

BRADFORD
(sort of singing) Ring and a ring and a ring and a ring --"

MONICA
(singing) "When I call --"

BRADFORD
(singing) "Looooove..."

MONICA
(singing) "Looooove...."

(Bradford and Monica stand close to each other. They smile. Bradford returns to slowly flipping through the album. Lights fade to black. End play.)

Devon & Kedzie:
Thillens Stadium

By Lonnie Carter

Copyright 2011 by Lonnie Carter. All rights reserved. CAUTION: Professionals and amateurs are hereby warned that *Devon & Kedzie: Thillens Stadium* is subject to a royalty. They are fully protected by the copyright laws of the United States of America and of all countries covered by the international Copyright Union (included the Dominion of Canada and the rest of the British Commonwealth), the Berne Convention, the Pan-American Copyright Convention and the University Copyright Convention, as well as all rights, including professional and amateur stage rights, motion picture, recitation, lecturing, public reading, radio broadcasting, television, video or sound recording, all other forms of mechanical or electronic reproduction, such as CD-ROM, CD-I, DVD, information storage and retrieval systems and photocopying, and the rights of translation into foreign languages, are strictly reserved. Particular emphasis is laid upon the matter of readings, permission for which must be secured in writing.

Required royalties must be paid every time this play is performed before any audience, whether or not it is presented for profit and whether or not admission is charged. To obtain stock and amateur performance rights, you must contact:

> Lonnie Carter
> PO Box 373
> Falls Village, CT 06031
> 860-824-8011

Playwright Biography

Lonnie Carter's play *The Romance of Magno Rubio*, winner of eight Obies in 2003 and part of the Victory Gardens 2004–2005 season, played an extended run in Honolulu at the Kumu Kahua Theatre in the spring of 2008. The 2007 production of *Magno*, by the Ma-Yi Theater Company at the Culture Project in NYC, opened the first National Asian-American Theater Festival. This production was subsequently invited to open the L.A. Latino Theater Festival at the L.A. Theater Center, then traveled to Bucharest and Sibiu, Romania to be part of the Sibiu International Theater Festival in June 2008. *Organizing Abraham Lincoln*, optioned by the Guthrie Theater and the Playwrights' Center in 2005, was performed at Temple University as part of a union fund-raising drive for striking Embassy Suites workers in Philadelphia this past spring. *Hawking* is about the last day on earth of Stephen Hawking. Victory Gardens produced his play *The Lost Boys (and Girl) of Sudan*. A graduate of Marquette University and the Yale School of Drama, he is a Victory Gardens Playwrights' Ensemble member and an alum of New Dramatists.

Acknowledgments

Devon & Kedzie: Thillens Stadium premiered as part of The Chicago Landmark Project in June 2011. It was directed by Jen Ellison with the following cast:

BILLY POWELL III	Destin Teamer
LONNIE CARTER	Kevin Woodrow

Cast
BILLY POWELL III, 12 years old, African-American
LONNIE CARTER, 11 years old, White

Both boys wear Chicago Cubs uniforms.

Setting
Thillens Stadium, Devon and Kedzie, Chicago.

Time
Late August, 1954.

Destin Teamer and Kevin Woodrow in *Devon & Kedzie: Thillens Stadium*

The Chicago Landmark Project
June – July, 2011
Produced by Theatre Seven of Chicago
Photo by Amanda Clifford

Devon & Kedzie: Thillens Stadium
by Lonnie Carter

      BILLY POWELL III
Last game.

      LONNIE
No.

      BILLY POWELL III
One more time.

      LONNIE
I'm ready.

      BILLY POWELL III
You're not ready. You never ready.

      LONNIE
I'm ready.

      BILLY POWELL III
I'm going to wipe you out.

      LONNIE
You and who? Tommy Thillens? Elliot Josephson? Paulie Biebel?

      BILLY POWELL III
Paulie on the team because his uncle the announcer. Paulie last chosen number 25. What your number? Seventeen? Come on, tell me.

      LONNIE
I don't know.

      BILLY POWELL III
Twenty-four. Next to last ahead of Paulie whose uncle announces the games. And Elliot? He got some talent. And Tommy got an arm, roaming center field. Doesn't matter his old man and uncle own the place, that's what my dad says. He got talent.

LONNIE
That's what my dad says.

BILLY POWELL III
Your dad; my dad.
Twenty-four? Well, you got some…talent.

LONNIE
My mom; your mom.
I got some talent. And you will see it on dis PLAY. To-DAY.
And tomorrow. You know tomorrow?

BILLY POWELL III
I know tomorrow?

LONNIE
Picnic.

BILLY POWELL III
What picnic?

LONNIE
You know. It's been in the works for weeks. Your parents. My parents. Us?

BILLY POWELL III
O, yeah, I heard them say something.

LONNIE
We'll bring Russell's.

BILLY POWELL III
Russell's?

LONNIE
I thought you lived on the South Side. The best pork in all Chicago.

BILLY POWELL III
I doubt you know your pork, sonny.

LONNIE
You'll see.

BILLY POWELL III
I'm going to wipe you out. You got Paulie on your side. Twenty-four and twenty-five, no whinin' from the intertwinin'. Tommy, Elliot - don't need them.

LONNIE
You going to start or not?

BILLY POWELL III
Hold on to your cap, boy.
Larry Doby. Newark Eagles. July 5, 1947. Cleveland Indians.

LONNIE
Jackie Robinson. Kansas City Monarchs. April 15, 1947. Brooklyn Dodgers.

BILLY POWELL III
Monte Irvin. Mr. Murder. Newark Eagles. July 8, 1949. New York Giants.
Roy Campanella said Mr. Murder best all'round player he ever saw.

LONNIE
Campy sees Jackie the best all'round player he ever saw every day.

BILLY POWELL III
James Thomas Cool Papa Bell. So fast he could steal first base. From first to third and no one ever saw him cross second. Quick as a wink, fast as a blink

LONNIE
Jack Roosevelt Robinson, Born: January 31, 1919 in Cairo, GA
College: University of California, Los Angeles.

BILLY POWELL III
College? Hell, Satchel Paige said, "If Cool Papa had known about colleges or if colleges had known about The Tan Cheetah, Jesse Owens would have looked like he was walking."

LONNIE
Jackie Robinson. Rookie of the year 1947.

BILLY POWELL III
Henry Louis Aaron. Bad Henry. Indianapolis Clowns. Willie Mays. Say Hey. Minneapolis Millers. Ernie Banks, Such a nice day; let's play two. Kansas City Monarchs. Ernie going to be Mr. Cub. Just you watch.

LONNIE
Most Valuable Player 1949.

BILLY POWELL III
Cool P many times scored from first on a bunt. Jackie ever do that?

LONNIE
Lots of times.

BILLY POWELL III
My father says there are lots of ball players better than your Jackie.

LONNIE
My Jackie? Thought he was our Jackie.

BILLY POWELL III
Maybe so.

LONNIE
You going to play Pony League?

BILLY POWELL III
Pony League?

LONNIE
Pony League. Thirteen, fourteen.

BILLY POWELL III
There ain't no Pony League where I live.

LONNIE
There ain't no Thillens where you live. I mean, you live on the South Side –

BILLY POWELL III
I know where I live.

LONNIE
So you mean you're not going to play? Thirteen and you're going to quit?

BILLY POWELL III
You got another year here, say hey, eleven. I'm twelve, I'm one and done.

LONNIE
You're a great pitcher. You're not done.

BILLY POWELL III
Maybe I'll wait a couple of years and play in the Negro Leagues.

LONNIE
They're not still going to be around. I bet -

BILLY POWELL III
You probably win that bet. My Dad says nobody goes to see them any more. Everybody wants to see our Jackie.

LONNIE
And Newk and Campy and Junior.

BILLY POWELL III
That's the point. But, I'm the only one here.

LONNIE
Well, we're still having our picnic, aren't we?

BILLY POWELL III
I guess. Is that what your folks say?

LONNIE
End of the season. We play the last game tonight and then tomorrow we have a picnic. We'll meet you at that park near where you live. My dad says he knows that park. Bring your glove. Our dads say they'll play too.

BILLY POWELL III
Is that what our Dads said?

LONNIE
And our Moms will bring the food. My Mom makes great fried chicken and potato salad.

BILLY POWELL III
My Mom makes that too. And sweet potato pie.

LONNIE
What's that?

BILLY POWELL III
O, sonny, you got a lot to learn.
Now what about this Russell's?

LONNIE
We'll bring that too. You'll see.
And our Moms will maybe have a fried chicken cook-off.

BILLY POWELL III
I guess we won't have a sweet potato pie cook-off.

LONNIE
I heard them talking about special ingredients.

BILLY POWELL III
You heard our moms talking about what?

LONNIE
They were talking about our picnic.

BILLY POWELL III
I don't eavesdrop.

LONNIE
I don't eavesdrop. They talked about it. I heard them. Couldn't miss it. You must have heard them too. And my Dad will bring some beer, if I know him. Your Dad drink beer?

BILLY POWELL III
Yeah, my Dad drinks beer.

LONNIE
My dad drinks beer when he paints. He says, Evelyn, I need beer for this paint.

BILLY POWELL III
My dad drinks beer.

LONNIE
My dad paints a lot. Sometimes the whole house three four times a year.

BILLY POWELL III
Maybe your dad can come by and paint my house. My house can use a little paint.

LONNIE
Well, he might do that. For some beer and stuff. We'll see about that.

BILLY POWELL III
Yeah, we'll see about that. Sure 'nuf.

LONNIE
We'll have a picnic and eat some great food and our Moms will talk and our Dads -

BILLY POWELL III and LONNIE
Will drink beer.

BILLY POWELL III
Last game. You warming me up or what?

LONNIE
You can come back next year and watch me play.

BILLY POWELL III
I'll be too busy playing Pony League.

LONNIE
Tonight I can feel it. I'm going to run so fast you won't even see me cross second.

BILLY POWELL III
That's Cool Papa. I'm Cool Papa. You're Jackie.

LONNIE
I'm Jackie. You're Cool Papa. Is that OK with you?

BILLY POWELL III
Is it OK with me? What do you think?

LONNIE
What do you mean, what do I think? You trying to start a fight?

BILLY POWELL III
No, man. No fight. You throw a good game. I like your game.

LONNIE
I like your game. You're a lot better than me.

BILLY POWELL III
For twenty-four, you're a pretty good guy.

LONNIE

Jackie number forty-two.

BILLY POWELL

You in reverse. Come on, warm me up. Last game, sonny. And then we got our picnic to go to. We'll lay out some bases in that park. Yeah, that's what we'll do alright. But right now tomorrow can wait.

LONNIE

It can wait 'til I steal home from first on a bunt.

BILLY POWELL III

Alright, already. Warm me up, will you, Mr. Forty-two.?

LONNIE

Yes sir, Mr. Seventeen.

(End Play.)

Honore & Milwaukee: Una Mae's Freak Boutique

By Brooke Berman

Copyright 2011 by Brooke Berman. All rights reserved. CAUTION: Professionals and amateurs are hereby warned that *Honore & Milwaukee: Una Mae's Freak Boutique* is subject to a royalty. They are fully protected by the copyright laws of the United States of America and of all countries covered by the international Copyright Union (included the Dominion of Canada and the rest of the British Commonwealth), the Berne Convention, the Pan-American Copyright Convention and the University Copyright Convention, as well as all rights, including professional and amateur stage rights, motion picture, recitation, lecturing, public reading, radio broadcasting, television, video or sound recording, all other forms of mechanical or electronic reproduction, such as CD-ROM, CD-I, DVD, information storage and retrieval systems and photocopying, and the rights of translation into foreign languages, are strictly reserved. Particular emphasis is laid upon the matter of readings, permission for which must be secured in writing.

Required royalties must be paid every time this play is performed before any audience, whether or not it is presented for profit and whether or not admission is charged. To obtain stock and amateur performance rights, you must contact:

> The Gersh Agency, c/o Seth Glewen
> 41 Madison Avenue
> 33rd Floor
> New York, NY 10010

Playwright Biography
Brooke Berman has had plays produced and developed across the US at theaters including: Primary Stages, The Second Stage, Steppenwolf, The Play Company, Soho Rep, Williamstown Theater Festival, Naked Angels, MCC, New Dramatists, New Georges, WET, SPF, The Hourglass Group, The Bay Area Playwrights Foundation and the Eugene O'Neill Theater Center. In the UK, her work has been developed at The Royal Court Theatre, The National Theatre Studio and Pentabus. Her plays are published by Broadway Play Publishing, Playscripts, Backstage Books and Smith & Kraus. Brooke is the recipient of a Berilla Kerr Award, a Helen Merrill Award, two Francesca Primus Awards, two LeCompte du Nuoy awards and a commissioning grant from the National Foundation for Jewish Culture. She recently completed a seven-year residency at New Dramatists, where she served on the Board of Directors and developed countless plays. She has received support for her work from the MacDowell Colony and the Corporation of Yaddo and commissions from Arielle Tepper Productions and Childrens Theatre Company in Minneapolis. Her memoir *No Place Like Home* was published by Random House in 2010. More information is available at: www.brookeberman.net.

Acknowledgments
Honore & Milwaukee: Una Mae's Freak Boutique premiered as part of The Chicago Landmark Project in June 2011. It was directed by Megan Shuchman with the following cast:

CARMEN	Dana Black
KRISTIN	Jessica Thigpen

Cast
CARMEN
KRISTIN

Setting
Una Mae's.

Time
Now.

Dana Black and Jessica Thigpen in *Honore & Milwaukee: Una Mae's Freak Boutique*

The Chicago Landmark Project
June – July, 2011
Produced by Theatre Seven of Chicago
Photo by Amanda Clifford

Honore & Milwaukee: Una Mae's Freak Boutique
by Brooke Berman

(A hipster resale clothing boutique full of garments that only a Fashionista Art Rebel or Tavi Gevlinson could love. Everything here is gently used and of chic label-whore origin.

Behind the counter, a young woman – late 20's, strangely dyed hair and some noticeable tattoos, sorts through a bag. She is on the phone.)

CARMEN
I can probably take the Norma Kamali. What's the fabric? Are the shoulder pads detachable? *(impressed despite herself)* Nice.
Well, I'm not making any promises – You still have to bring it in so I can inspect its ass. But… could work. What else have you got?

(She listens.)

Maybe.
Maybe.

(Grinds to a halt.)

No.
We don't take "Gap." *('Gap' should sound like it's a dirty word.)* We don't take Banana. We don't take Old Navy. Ever. I steer clear of anything you can get at The Water Tower. No Forever 21, no Zara, no Ann Taylor Loft, no exceptions.

Gunne Sax? Yeah, that moment came and went. I mean, we all thought it was going to be this totally ironic take-back the prairie night, but do you really want to walk around looking like Holly Hobby? I don't.
Listen – bring your stuff in, I'll take a look. That's the most I can promise. I have to see it before I can say for sure. The Kamali sounds fierce.

When am I here?
Babycakes. I'm always here.

(Another woman, roughly Carmen's age, has entered the store, with a small bag of clothes – 2 items. She looks around, sort of taking the whole thing in. And when Carmen gets off the phone –)

KRISTIN
This used to be –

CARMEN
Well it's not anymore. And we probably don't have what you want.

KRISTIN
This whole neighborhood's –

CARMEN
I know.

KRSTIN
Did they close? The other place? I liked them. I used to live here. I mean, not HERE, but here in Chicago, on the North side. The North East side. We never really came this far West –

CARMEN
It's Damen. Not the frontier.

KRISTIN
Sure. But when I was a kid, when I was living here, when I was a teenager, whatever, we sort of always hung out around –

CARMEN
Lincoln Park.

KRISTIN
Yes! So this is –

CARMEN
-- already come and gone. The New Bohemia of it all. Now it's just a neighborhood like any other. More hipsters. But not so whatever, vanguard.

KRISTIN
I don't live in Chicago anymore.

CARMEN
Good for you.

KRISTIN
I have clothes to sell. Vintage.

CARMEN
Put them over there. I'll get to them.

KRISTIN
Is there a wait?

CARMEN
There is.

KRISTIN
There's no one else in the store.

CARMEN
Your point?

KRISTIN
Just that… There's no one else in the --

CARMEN
I'm in the middle of something.

KRISTIN
I'll wait.

(She sits on a bench. She stares at Carmen. Carmen tries to ignore her. This is hard. Grudgingly, Carmen starts to look through the bag of clothes that Kristin has brought with her – it's a very small bag with a select, few items. Carmen lifts up a vintage robe in excellent condition. She inspects the thing, taking care to look at its label, which obviously impresses her.)

CARMEN
This is —

KRISTIN
I know.

CARMEN
Vintage?

KRISTIN
1979.

CARMEN
I didn't know they did robes.

KRISTIN
They don't anymore.

(Carmen inspects the robe.)

CARMEN
How much you want?

KRISTIN
I don't know.

CARMEN
Make me an offer.

KRISTIN
Two hundred?

CARMEN
No way.

KRISTIN
Why'd you ask?

CARMEN
It's how I do business.

KRISTIN
But if you already knew you had a cap, I mean, why ask me to — when you already have some notion of --

CARMEN
One twenty five.

KRISTIN
It was my mother's.

CARMEN
Why is that useful to me?

KRISTIN
Well. It isn't. It's just --

CARMEN
You want to hold onto it out of some displaced notion of loyalty or guilt, maybe, and not make the cash? Because gentrified or not, no one around here is gonna pop two hundred bucks on an old robe.

KRISTIN
I remember her wearing it.

CARMEN
Which means no sale? Fine. Take the robe home.

KRISTIN
I had it dry-cleaned. And it fits me. But I can't wear it. When I try, and believe me, I have tried, but when I try, I just feel --

CARMEN
Ghosts.

KRISTIN
Yes!

CARMEN
Old things have ghosts.

KRISTIN
When I put it on, I feel… her expectation.

CARMEN
What'd she expect?

KRISTIN
A certain kind of life.

CARMEN
What'd she get?

KRISTIN
A different kind of life. *(Kristin confides.)* She bought it for a man.

CARMEN
And he cheated.

KRISTIN
How did you know that? Are you a robe-whisperer?

CARMEN
They always cheat. That's how it goes wrong. They cheat.

KRISTIN
Well, he did.

CARMEN
And you can feel it in the robe.

KRISTIN
Is that crazy?

(Carmen picks up the robe, smells it, presses it to her face.)

CARMEN
No. I feel it too. Sell it to me for 125 and be free.

KRISTIN
I think it's worth more.

CARMEN
Do you? You want to go all eBay? Do it yourself? You got user ratings and all that? I bet you're like a real eBay Wiz.

KRISTIN
That label is worth something.

CARMEN
To fashion people. Sure. But to Wicker Park hipsters? They don't give a flying fuck about this label. Excuse my French. And moreover, it's a little... *(she makes a face)*

KRISTIN
A little what?

CARMEN
Demure.

KRISTIN
You make that sound like a bad thing.

CARMEN
Who wants a demure robe in this fabric? This is not demure fabric. This is Joan Crawford fabric. If you want demure, wear cotton, flannel, muslin. Not tafetta. Tafetta has a whole other connotation.

(Kristin thinks about it. The girl does have a point.)

KRISTIN
You know a lot.

CARMEN
It's my job.

KRISTIN
Are you a designer?

CARMEN
I'm a collector. An aficionado. You want the 125?

KRISTIN
How about the cape?

CARMEN
What cape?

KRISTIN
There's a cape.

(Carmen digs in the bag, and sure enough, there is a black velvet cape.)

CARMEN
Whoa. Holy Harry Potter, Batman.

KRISTIN
I thought I'd wear that too.

CARMEN
On Halloween maybe. Or at your next Wiccan ritual. When you try to make peace with your dead mother and her expectations.

(Ouch. That kind of hurt. Kristin winces.)

CARMEN
Sorry. Look, okay, I'll take them both. I need a valid ID in order to do the paperwork. *(Beat.)* You're not going to get a better offer unless you know someone in the vintage business.

KRISTIN
You're right. Okay. It's probably, I shouldn't – okay.

(Kristin hands Carmen her driver's license. Carmen looks at it, suspicious and sort of – having a moment.)

CARMEN
Kristin Sadoski?

(Kristin nods.)

CARMEN

You live in LA.

(Kristin nods again. Carmen is still holding her driver's license.)

CARMEN

But you're from here. You went to high school here. You grew up on Orchard.

KRISTIN

Do I know you?

CARMEN

You made out with my boyfriend.

KRISTIN

Excuse me!?

CARMEN

I don't have proof. The evidence is circumstantial. But I have good instincts. And from the circumstantial evidence and a couple of things his friends have said… I'm pretty sure you made out with my boyfriend, drunk dialed him a few times the summer before last, and probably you've seen him on this trip.

KRISTIN

Look, I'm sure you have me mixed up with someone else.

CARMEN

Stu. My boyfriend is Stu. From high school.

KRISTIN

Oh.

CARMEN

Exactly. Whore!

KRISTIN
We went to high school together.

CARMEN
Yes. I know.

KRISTIN
We made out in high school. But not after high school. Just IN high school. And not even senior year.

CARMEN
Apparently it was very meaningful.

KRISTIN
Awkward.

CARMEN
This? Or going down on Stu in high school?

KRISTIN
Both. What's your name?

CARMEN
Carmen.

(Kristin looks blank.)

CARMEN
He didn't mention me.

(Kristin shakes her head. No. "Carmen" was not mentioned.)

CARMEN
So have you seen him? On this trip?

(Kristin shakes her head no.)

CARMEN
Good.

KRISTIN

The last time was – I guess, here. In this neighborhood. There was a party. That summer you're talking about. But I really don't remember… I mean, we fooled around a long, long time ago. Like, a REALLY long time ago. And Stu never mentioned a serious girlfriend, I mean, when we spoke. I mean, the last time I saw him… or really, any time I've ever seen him, I can't recall a serious girlfriend. And I seriously doubt anyone made out. With anyone. I'd remember that. I would! Really! Wouldn't I?

CARMEN

You should go. Take your ghost-robe and your Harry Potter cape and… be gone!

KRISTIN

Are you in love with him? I know that's none of my business but… Are you?

CARMEN

"What's love got to do with it? … What's love but a second-hand emotion?"

KRISTIN

Because… I think he's a douchebag. If he's never mentioned you. To someone like me.

CARMEN

"Who needs a heart when a heart can be broken?"

KRISTIN

Are you still together?

CARMEN

Which part of "Be Gone" don't you understand? *(She takes aim at Kristin with an imaginary gun or bow and arrow.)* No. We are very recently not together. No. Happy? Gonna go text him or something?

KRISTIN

Take my mom's things. Just take them. No money. A gift. Not out of guilt. I didn't do anything. That I remember. But just because. Because. You loved and lost or whatever. And because Stu and I grew up together, and – between us, I think he's kind of a douchebag even if I did make out with him in Tracey Yardlin's basement and even if it's entirely possible that I did again and don't remember because of the whole, you know, dead parent thing and the weird aftermath of all of THAT. I don't even know why. But please. Just take –

(She pushes the bag towards Carmen.)

CARMEN

He liked your mom.

(This was unexpected.)

KRISTIN

Yes. He did. They –

CARMEN

He talked about her. When she died. I remember. He said she was always –

KRISTIN

Very warm. She was. Everyone thought so. Unless they were married to her. Then, I think, it was more complicated.

CARMEN

He said she gave him a chance.

KRISTIN

Yes. And his own parents…..

CARMEN

Didn't.

KRISTIN

No.

CARMEN
I'm sorry. About her. For your loss. You know.

KRISTIN
Thank you. *(Beat.)* It's very strange being back. Now. Alone.

(Kristin pushes the bag further towards Carmen.)

Please will you take my stuff? You don't even have to pay me.

(Carmen takes the bag.)

CARMEN
The ghosts want me to pay you.

KRISTIN
Yeah?

CARMEN
They think you need the money.

(Kristin looks relieved. Carmen hands Kristin one hundred and fifty dollars.)

CARMEN
Here. I'm throwing in 25 ~~for the Harry Potter cape~~. Your mom says to go buy yourself a lipstick. And a decent meal. And to call your cousins. Do you have cousins?

(Kristin nods.)

CARMEN
Call them.

KRISTIN
Thank you.

(It's as if the two women are about to have a moment, but Carmen won't allow such sentimentality in her store.)

CARMEN

You can go now.

KRISTIN

But –

CARMEN

The past has nothing for you. And really, neither do I. Bye!

(Kristin leaves the store. Carmen watches after her. Then, Carmen picks up the phone and places a call.)

CARMEN

What's up, Lovely Face? It's Carmen.
Any chance you want a seriously high end vintage robe? Five hundred.
I could get six for it, but I want to pass it on to someone who'll really appreciate its quality.
Yeah? Great. I'll hold onto it for you.
Behind the counter. In the "Reserve" section.
It's got good energy. A ghost, the good kind of ghost, like a mom, a mother, a blessing attached.
For reals.
I can feel it.

(End play.)

63rd & Kedzie:
Arab American Community Center

By Jamil Khoury

Copyright 2011 by Jamil Khoury. All rights reserved. CAUTION: Professionals and amateurs are hereby warned that *63rd & Kedzie: Arab American Community Center* is subject to a royalty. They are fully protected by the copyright laws of the United States of America and of all countries covered by the international Copyright Union (included the Dominion of Canada and the rest of the British Commonwealth), the Berne Convention, the Pan-American Copyright Convention and the University Copyright Convention, as well as all rights, including professional and amateur stage rights, motion picture, recitation, lecturing, public reading, radio broadcasting, television, video or sound recording, all other forms of mechanical or electronic reproduction, such as CD-ROM, CD-I, DVD, information storage and retrieval systems and photocopying, and the rights of translation into foreign languages, are strictly reserved. Particular emphasis is laid upon the matter of readings, permission for which must be secured in writing.

Required royalties must be paid every time this play is performed before any audience, whether or not it is presented for profit and whether or not admission is charged. To obtain stock and amateur performance rights, you must contact:

>Jamil Khoury
>Artistic Director, Silk Road Theatre Project
>jamil@srtp.org

Playwright Biography

Jamil Khoury is a playwright and Founding Artistic Director of Silk Road Theatre Project (www.srtp.org). In 2010, he received the prestigious 3Arts Artist Award for Playwriting. Khoury's plays focus on Middle Eastern themes and questions of Diaspora. He is particularly interested in the intersections of culture, national identity, sexuality, and class. Khoury's short play, *WASP: White Arab Slovak Pole*, has been produced as a video play and will be released in 2011. His play *Precious Stones* won Gay Chicago Magazine's 2003 After Dark Award for Outstanding New Work and has been performed in ten cities across the U.S.

Acknowledgments

63rd & Kedzie: Arab American Community Center premiered as part of The Chicago Landmark Project in June 2011. It was directed by Brian Golden with the following cast:

HANAN	Amira Sabbagh
HEIDI	Leslie Frame

Cast

HANAN, a 30-something Arab American woman
HEIDI, a 30-something Caucasian woman

Setting

A health club in downtown Chicago.

Time

Present.

Amira Sabbagh and Leslie Frame in *63rd & Kedzie: Arab American Community Center*

The Chicago Landmark Project
June – July, 2011
Produced by Theatre Seven of Chicago
Photo by Amanda Clifford

63rd & Kedzie: Arab American Community Center
by Jamil Khoury

HANAN
Okay. What's with the silent treatment?

HEIDI
Silent treatment?

HANAN
I finally get you down to 63rd and Kedzie, for an evening of fun and frolicking at the Arab Community Center, and you don't say a word.

HEIDI
I had a good time. You need to stay focused on your balance.

HANAN
I am focused. You left early. You barely said goodbye. Did I do something wrong?

HEIDI
No. You were talking to your friends. You had family there. I didn't want to intrude.

HANAN
You were my guest, Heidi!

HEIDI
We're doing twelve reps of each set.

HANAN
I know what I'm doing. You're dodging the question.

HEIDI
It was a new experience for me. It was, I don't know, it was different. I'm still processing.

HANAN
Different as in good different or weird different or get me the hell away from all these crazy Arabs different?

HEIDI
I was really touched when you invited me. It meant a great deal to me. I'd never been to an Arab event before.

HANAN
I wanted you to experience my world. I see you here in the gym, you know, we're always in your world.

HEIDI
Come on, this gym is as much yours as it is mine.

HANAN
What do you mean you're still processing?

HEIDI
I loved the music, the dancing. The food, my God, was delicious!

HANAN
But?

HEIDI
I thought it would have been better without the politics. It got a little heated for my tastes.

HANAN
The politics?

HEIDI
Reaches next. 15 to each side. I had an issue with that woman who was, I don't know, the MC for the evening.

HANAN
Suheila?

HEIDI
Is she a friend of yours?

HANAN
More like a friend of my parents, but I thought Suheila did a wonderful job. She was funny. She told jokes. She kept the evening moving along, which, believe me, in my community is no small feat.

HEIDI
Look, I don't want to offend you or anything, I just...

HANAN
Heidi. No one has seen me fall on my ass more than you have, not even my parents. Speak your mind, woman!

HEIDI
What was all that stuff about "Stop America's racist war against our people!"

HANAN
Come on. Arabs are very hyperbolic.

HEIDI
That woman had a lot of anger in her.

HANAN
Okay, Arab World 101. U.S. policy in the Middle East sees three things – Israel, Arab dictators, and oil. America happens to love all three. As for the Arab people, eh, not so interested. "You got hopes and dreams kid? Sorry. Tough luck."

HEIDI
I'm not defending U.S. foreign policy, okay, but for a moment there I forgot what country I was in.

HANAN
Somewhere between Midway Airport and Abu Ghraib! In the Arab world. It's all about fiery speeches and empty rhetoric.

HEIDI
Fiery speeches incite action.

HANAN
Actually, in the Arab community, we prefer words to action.

HEIDI
Good job. Rest. The way Suheila would say the word "America." With such utter contempt and disdain.

HANAN
It was probably her accent that threw you.

HEIDI
No. And it wasn't just her. The other speakers…"American," "Americans" were like bad words. And I'm standing there thinking - they're talking about me.

HANAN
I'm sorry, were we at the same event Saturday night?

HEIDI
As the only white girl in the room, honestly speaking, I didn't feel safe.

HANAN
What? Why? People were thrilled that I brought you. They kept asking about you. Who's that pretty American girl?

HEIDI
How was I to know? They were speaking to you in Arabic. People were pointing at me and smiling, in this like really odd way.

HANAN
It's the culture. We're not terribly discreet about…you know, pointing. Finish with the Around the Worlds?

HEIDI
Your favorite. Why was I being referred to as "the American girl?" Aren't all of us Americans?

HANAN
Of course we are, but for Arabs, you know, Americans are white people.

HEIDI
White people?

HANAN
I was bragging to everyone about you. I'm proud of you. I kept telling people, "that's her, that's Heidi, my personal trainer, the one who helped me lose all the weight, helped me reverse my diabetes."

HEIDI
Oh, that's so sweet of you, Hanan. My God, I feel terrible for having said anything...

HANAN
Don't. I need to hear it. It's so easy to get all insular and stop seeing how others perceive you. This is helpful.

HEIDI
Listen, the weight loss, the diabetes. That's your accomplishment. You did the work.

HANAN
Yes, but you helped me, big time. I'm indebted to you.

HEIDI
You shouldn't. I'm doing my job.

HANAN
But you went above and beyond. You saved my life, girlfriend.

HEIDI
I'm just happy I can provide you support. It's why I'm a trainer. Besides, you give me bookoo bragging rights, Ms. Fitness sensation!

HANAN
Now that's more like it.

HEIDI

Take a rest.

HANAN

It's funny. People kept asking "is that American girl on our side? Does she feel for us?"

HEIDI

What did they mean am I on their side?

HANAN

Feelings in the Arab community are very raw these days. People feel vulnerable and insecure. You can't blame 'em. Being on the defensive all the time...

HEIDI

Not to sound callous, but striking an ardently anti-American tone doesn't exactly endear people to your cause.

HANAN

There was nothing anti-American. Granted, Suheila could have been more diplomatic. She was a bit unpolished and uncouth. Not to mention unfiltered.

HEIDI

Now the other direction.

HANAN

I'm in Beitounia, in the West Bank, visiting family. My six year old nephew Ramzi hands me a bunch of "rubber bullets." Actually they're rubber coated metal bullets that the Israelis shoot at young children. He hands me the bullets, this adorable little boy, and he says, "Auntie, can you please tell America to stop sending these?" Turns out they're made in Pennsylvania!

HEIDI

Look, I'm horrified at what Israel does. And I really feel for your family there. I'm also horrified at what Arab governments do to their own people.

HANAN
No argument there.

HEIDI
But I saw plenty of Arab flags at the cultural center, but not one American flag.

HANAN
Yes, and there should be an American flag. I've complained about that myself.

HEIDI
I kept wondering, where exactly is the American in Arab American?

HANAN
It was an event celebrating our heritage! I'd say that's pretty American. You wear green on St. Patrick's Day.

HEIDI
My parent's raised us to be fiercely proud of being American. We were taught to love this country. And not uncritically mind you.

HANAN
Great! I love this country too! And I'm damn critical of it.

HEIDI
I'm not talking about you, Hanan. I don't see you as one of them.

HANAN
One of them? What is that?

HEIDI
I'm sorry. It didn't come out right. I guess what I'm trying to say is…I see you as American first.

HANAN
Sure, of course, but…you know, I am damn proud of who I am. Okay. I'm American. I'm Arab. I'm Palestinian. I'm Muslim. I'm a

Chicagoan. I'm an accountant. I'm a piano player. I'm an amateur astronomer. I'm a wannabe jock... *(both laugh)*

HEIDI
And I'm a whole lot of things as well. But I don't hyphenate my Americanness.

HANAN
Well, you and I don't walk in the same shoes now, do we?

HEIDI
One of the speakers at the event, an older man, he went on and on about all the "horrible things" the "criminal Americans" are doing to *our people* in Iraq. Criminal Americans? Do you realize that right now, as we speak, my cousin Brian is in Iraq risking his life trying to prevent Iraqis from slaughtering each other?

HANAN
That was one man's opinion. He doesn't represent me, and he certainly doesn't represent the entire Arab community.

HEIDI
You know what I wanted to say to that guy? "Whose side are you on, buddy? If we're then enemy, then get the hell out of here!"

HANAN
America – love it or leave it! You're not coming out as a red neck, are you?

HEIDI
Look, we're starting to hurt each other's feelings. We should probably end this conversation. I'll put the bosu away.

HANAN
Why are you picking on Arabs all of sudden? What, we don't have enough enemies as it is?

HEIDI
I'm hardly your enemy. But I bet if I took a poll Saturday night of "those Americans"...

HANAN
Stop! I was born here. But my parents, and all their friends, they're from the old country. It is hard being an immigrant, Heidi. Real hard. So before you start asking anyone to take a loyalty oath...

HEIDI
A man grabs a microphone and screams "First Israel, then America." Gee, I wonder what he means?

HANAN
I don't remember that ever being said. In fact, it wasn't.

HEIDI
Oh, it most certainly was. And no one batted an eye.

HANAN
You know, with all due respect...I thought you were a liberal? How about a little empathy? Those speakers, the ones who so riled you up, those people have horror stories. They are people who fled for their lives. Palestinians, Iraqis, Lebanese, Syrians...

HEIDI
Yes, and America gave them a home where they could be safe and free and prosperous. Don't forget to stretch those abdominals.

(Heidi helps her stretch her core.)

HANAN
You think if you moved to China tomorrow, and spent the rest of your life living there, that you'd stop being American. Stop speaking English? Stop hanging out with other Americans? Sure, you might learn Chinese? You might even master the culture, try and fit in, but you'll never be accepted as Chinese.

HEIDI
I'll never be Chinese because being Chinese is an ethnic identity. The great thing about this country is that anyone can become an American. It's not about blood lines. It's about ideals and beliefs and shared values. That's the beauty of the American melting pot.

HANAN
Yeah, well I don't want to be thrown into a pot to be melted! Okay. Give me the salad bowl any day over the melting pot. You're a tomato, I'm a green pepper, we're each unique, but we're part of the same, delicious salad.

HEIDI
Fine, let's be a salad bowl, but if the cucumber is always dissing the radish...

HANAN
It makes for one zesty, colorful salad!

HEIDI
(Laughs) You think all this exercise is short circuiting our brains?

HANAN
Could be, but at least we've got abs of steel!

HEIDI
(Looks at watch.) Oh gosh. I've got another client coming. We're still on for Wednesday morning, right.

HANAN
10:00am. We'll continue with the bosu?

HEIDI
Actually Wednesday I'd like us to do some machines. We'll need to focus on shoulders and back.

(End Play.)

Belmont & Western: Riverview Amusement Park

By Aaron Carter

Copyright 2011 by Aaron Carter. All rights reserved. CAUTION: Professionals and amateurs are hereby warned that *Belmont & Western: Riverview Amusemnt Park* is subject to a royalty. They are fully protected by the copyright laws of the United States of America and of all countries covered by the international Copyright Union (included the Dominion of Canada and the rest of the British Commonwealth), the Berne Convention, the Pan-American Copyright Convention and the University Copyright Convention, as well as all rights, including professional and amateur stage rights, motion picture, recitation, lecturing, public reading, radio broadcasting, television, video or sound recording, all other forms of mechanical or electronic reproduction, such as CD-ROM, CD-I, DVD, information storage and retrieval systems and photocopying, and the rights of translation into foreign languages, are strictly reserved. Particular emphasis is laid upon the matter of readings, permission for which must be secured in writing.

Required royalties must be paid every time this play is performed before any audience, whether or not it is presented for profit and whether or not admission is charged. To obtain stock and amateur performance rights, you must contact:

Aaron Carter
adcarter@gmail.com

Playwright Biography

Aaron Carter is a Chicago playwright, originally from Ohio. His paternal grandfather was a black Baptist preacher, his maternal grandparents were white vaudeville performers. The influence of his ancestors is seen in Aaron's work which focuses on race, faith, and obscure performance skills. His play in progress *Start Fair In the Common Race* was presented in a workshop production in the "What's Next Lab" at Next Theater. Aaron is also working on *The Book of Astaroth*, a commission made possible by the Wallace Foundation. *First Words*, produced by MPAACT, was nominated for a non-Equity Jeff Award and received a Black Theater Alliance Award. Other productions include *Panther Burn* (MPAACT), and *Swamp Baby* (Phase 3 Productions). His play *Iowa Akhbar* was workshopped as part of Leapfest 5 at Stage Left Theater. Aaron is the Literary Manager at Victory Gardens Theater. He also works as a new play developer and dramaturg for such companies as WordBRIDGE and the Kennedy Center American College Theater Festival.

Acknowledgments

Belmont & Western: Riverview Amusement Park premiered as part of The Chicago Landmark Project in June 2011. It was directed by Vance Smith with the following cast:

KAREN	Sam Bailey
HUNTER	Andrew Raia
ALVARO	Arthur Soria
ELIJAH	Desmond Gray

Cast
KAREN
HUNTER
ALVARO
ELIJAH

Setting
The site of Chicago's Riverview Amusement Park, now nothing more than crumbling concrete foundations overgrown by a thin urban wood near a bike path.

Time
3am-ish.

Arthur Soria, Andrew Raia, Sam Bailey and Desmond Gray in
Belmont & Western: Riverview Amusement Park

The Chicago Landmark Project
June – July, 2011
Produced by Theatre Seven of Chicago
Photo by Amanda Clifford

Belmont & Western: Riverview Amusement Park
by Aaron Carter

(Two graffiti covered concrete benches form a shallow V. At the point of the V is the base of a small streetlight that illuminates the benches. A suggestion of a walking path. It's night. 3am-ish, or whatever hour it is when you're a teenager and you've snuck out of your home and met up with friends for no other reason than to celebrate the fact that you have snuck out of your home)

(Karen, a studious-looking black girl enters. She's followed closely by Hunter, a white kid. Alvaro, a light-skinned Latino, trails the pair. He's boooooooored.)

(Karen holds a book and some papers.)

KAREN
Can you believe it? It's like the bones of some ancient leviathan.

ALVARO
FUCK. MY. LIFE.

HUNTER
I thought we were going to be, like, in the parking lot?

KAREN
We met in the parking lot.

HUNTER
But there are more lights. The Toys R Us sign alone lights up a whole block.

ALVARO
What, you scared?

HUNTER
No. Just that, up front, there's like a whole fleet of cops. Don't you feel safer knowing that if shit went down, like a whole bunch of cops would be right there?

KAREN
No.

ALVARO
Shiiii, you know that's right.

(A little brown solidarity dap.)

HUNTER
Whatever. So, have you dated white guys?

ALVARO
Dude.

HUNTER
Like, in the past?

KAREN
You asking me out?

HUNTER
I uh- it's just. When you do shit like - *(maybe a gesture indicating the solidarity moment)* I'm not saying - I'm just wondering. If it's like a thing you don't do.

KAREN
Yeah Hunter. I've dated white guys.

HUNTER
Cool.

ALVARO
Oh Christ.

(Quiet. Hunter tries to regain some ground.)

HUNTER
So that crumbling concrete. That was like the boatslide?

KAREN
Hell yeah. That's the channel the boats ran in. The Chutes - not to be confused with the Pair O Chutes which was the aerial ride. 'bout where that antenna tower is.

HUNTER
You like just sat in a boat?

KAREN
Well yeah, but it was like a a log flume -

ALVARO
A what now?

KAREN
Y'all need to learn some history. There was like a sixty foot hill right where we were standing. The boats when shooting down this giant-ass hill, skimming across the water -

HUNTER
Oh, it was fast.

KAREN
Totally.

HUNTER
Like a water coaster.

KAREN
Now you feeling me. But the for real coaster was the Jetstream. There. No. There. Carousel was right over there. This whole path was like carnival games.

ALVARO
So, booths like where you pitch quarters on a dinner plate? Or like, where you like ping them ducks down and shit.

HUNTER
What you know about it?

ALVARO
Fuck you. I seen cartoons, man.

KAREN
Yeah, sure. Like that.

ALVARO
Cool. And where's the booth where they jab a red-hot needle through my junk? 'cause that would be more exciting than -

(Hunter grabs Alvaro and pulls him aside.)

HUNTER
What the hell? Wingman?

ALVARO
What?

KAREN
I can hear you idiots.

HUNTER
You know, "Hunter's cool. He's not a creep."

KAREN
Right, 'cause alone in the dark with two guys, that makes a girl feel safe.

ALVARO
Coming out here was her idea. Maybe it's your naughty bits we should be protecting.

KAREN
He wishes. Can we all just keep quiet?

(A bit of a silence.)

KAREN
I think the freak show was over there --

ALVARO
You're the freak show.

HUNTER
Ass-munch!

(Hunter grabs Alvaro and punches him hard in the arm.)

KAREN
Idiots.

HUNTER
But I'm defending you!

KAREN
(she might mean it a little...) Yeah. Thanks.

HUNTER
Why'd you invite me out here, anyway?

KAREN
I dunno, Riverview is important to me.

HUNTER
Why?

KAREN
Everything is so... Everything is so...

(A faint noise. It's odd. It's vaguely human. In a little while we will recognize it as people screaming as they ride a roller-coaster. But for now, it sounds as it has been echoed across a score of years.)

ALVARO
What the hell?

HUNTER
Maybe we should -

KAREN
People called it "A Kingdom of Magic." It seemed like, I dunno - I mean, yeah it was a con or whatever or cheap or dangerous, but

you could EXPERIENCE something for what you paid, not just go SHOP for something. It was like a purer time or whatever.

                    HUNTER

You believe that?

                    KAREN

Yes. No. It's nice to pretend that its true? But you got to ignore a whole lotta --

One of them carnie type games was a dunk tank they called the African Dip. Early on they called it Dunk The Nigger.

                    ALVARO

You shitting me.

                    KAREN

They paid this brother to sit up on the platform and shout at the people. Heckle em so they would pay up to dunk him down.

                    ALVARO

That is fuckin awesome. How I get that job? I'd sit up there being all, "Yo mama this, yo mama that" and they'd be all, "Nigga, what?" That is the shit right there!

                    KAREN

You're an idiot.

                    HUNTER

Asshole!

                    ALVARO

What? I'm brown. Besides, we're post-racial, bitch.

                    KAREN

Since when are you brown?

                    ALVARO

(with accent) Alvaro Mendez.

KAREN
Why you only claim color when you're saying stupid shit?

ALVARO
Whatever. I'm more brown than *Hunter* over here.

KAREN
Everyone's more brown than *Hunter*.

HUNTER
It's a family name, assholes.

ALVARO
Now white people are insulted when we call them white. I mean, what is that about? Them white pride idiots have kinda got a point.

(The sound again.)

HUNTER
Can we just go?

KAREN
Go ahead.

HUNTER
Look Karen, it's just I got this test tomorrow. We could maybe come back --

(Hunter's pathetic wheedling is undercut by Elijah bursting on the scene. Elijah's appearance is accompanied by a particularly loud instance of the sound. Elijah is black. He's also out of breath. And running, full tilt. He clips Karen and plows straight into Hunter. Elijah tumbles to the ground. We're probably noticing that he's dressed in strategically period neutral clothing. He's just shown up from 1967, but given how hip our little f-bomb-droppers are, his clothing probably doesn't look completely out of place. But of course, we don't know he's from 1967. Not yet. What we know right now is that a black teenager just rocketed into Hunter, and stumbled to the ground. Elijah gets to his feet - he is instantly apologetic.)

ELIJAH
I don't want no trouble. I didn't see ya standing there.

HUNTER
S'cool bro.

(He's edging away.)

ELIJAH
I just be on my way. Now I didn't see nothing, alright. I don't want no trouble.

HUNTER
Whatever, man.

(And Elijah is the hell outta there.)

ALVARO
What the fuck was that?

KAREN
You ain't never seen someone act polite before?

ALVARO
You think po-po was after him?

HUNTER
Come on. We're out.

(They turn, but Elijah is suddenly standing there again.)

ELIJAH
Have you gentlemen seen a man with a gun?

HUNTER
What??

(Elijah crosses, looks off where he originally entered.)

ELIJAH
About so tall. Brown hair. Coveralls, name tag. Waving a gun?

HUNTER
Guys? Guys?

ELIJAH
Just a pellet gun. Still, it stings.

ALVARO
We ain't seen nobody.

ELIJAH
Well good. Ok then -

(Elijah now faces the boys.)

ELIJAH
Now, you can blame my mama for this. Because me, I, Elijah --if it was up to me I'd be home by bestowing this here stuffed bear -- which I won fair and square-- on my sister. I say if a game is fixed it's only fair that I take my compensation in goods. But what I'm sayin' is if it were up to me, I'd be home right now.
But, ah, see, here's the thing. I was raised by my mama and all I can say is that I'd rather the girl came on with me.

ALVARO
Did you understand a fucking thing he just said?

HUNTER
Alright man, I'm not sure what you're on or whatever, but why don't you just go.

(Elijah musters his strength.)

ELIJAH
Mama, mama I hate you right now mama.

(Elijah advances on the men.)

ELIJAH
Well, let me ask you one last thing here then before we commence to the thing that seems to have become inevitable.

HUNTER
Uh... ok...

ELIJAH
After I finish kicking your asses here, can I have your word as upstanding white men that you will not gather up a mob of your people and visit your vengeance on my neighborhood or on the next random black man that you see?

HUNTER
Kicking our asses -

ALVARO
Who is this other white dude he's on about?

HUNTER AND KAREN
You are!

ELIJAH
Can we get back to where I'm saving you please?

HUNTER
Look, whacko, can you just get out of here alright? There's three of us, and there's one of you, so do the math, man.

ALVARO
That's real chivalrous, include the girl in the count of who's throwing down.

(Hunter shoves Alvaro.)

HUNTER
Fuck off, man!

(Alvaro shoves back.)

ALVARO

Give it up.

ELIJAH

Alirght, alright girl, now's our chance.

(Elijah grabs Karen. She resists.)

KAREN

Guys! Help!

(Alvaro and Hunter leave off beating on each other and advance on Elijah. They are interrupted by the freight train roar of a wooden roller coaster bearing down on them. It's loud. It's unlike anything they've heard.)

(Karen, Hunter, and Alvaro hit the deck. Elijah sits center, laughing.)

ELIJAH

Awww, shit people! Its gonna stay on the track.

Probably.

(He starts laughing again.)

ELIJAH

You all ain't ever been here before?

HUNTER

Here? What do you mean, here?

ELIJAH

The way them turns is, riders don't usually see you. People get up to all sorts of stuff under here. And I thought you was dangerous.

(Elijah laughs.)

HUNTER

Guys, let's just go, OK? This is - this ... we should just -

KAREN
What ah, what else you like about ... here?

ELIJAH
Well my sister, what's not to like? It's a kingdom of magic.

KAREN
Holy shit.

ELIJAH
Says right on the gate "Laugh Your Troubles Away." That's a motto I try to live. *(To Karen)* What's your favorite ride?

KAREN
I - uh. I always wanted to see Aladdin's Castle.

ELIJAH
I get by there. I got my route, though. I like to hit the Pair o Chutes first.

(As Elijah speaks, he conjures Riverview in the form of twinkle-light outlines that slowly fade into view.)

KAREN
What's it like? To actually ride it?

ELIJAH
It's like... it's like the air just scrub you clean. You drop through the air and all the dirt and grime and bad feelings just caked on your skin, they just come flaking off.

KAREN
I wish I could do that.

(Our trash-talking boys see the flesh and blood of Riverview. They are stunned, and a little scared.)

ELIJAH
Well, I'll take you.

KAREN
What do you do after that?

HUNTER
Oh my god.

ALVARO
No fucking way.

ELIJAH
I go on over Aladdin's Castle. It's a little scary, but it's scary good. So now I'm all jazzed and electrified so I gotta hit the boats to cool down a bit. But first I gotta find me a girl to go on those boats with me. What you say?

(Elijah takes a charmed Karen by the hand.)

KAREN
I don't. I don't have any, ah money.

ELIJAH
Come on, girl, why you talking money? You're with me, now. I'll treat you right.

KAREN
O.K.

HUNTER
Karen, are you seeing this?

ELIJAH
You ain't scared, is you?

KAREN
No.

ELIJAH
Cause you get scared, it's OK if you wanna grab on to me. Them boats get awful fast. I ain't mind at all.

KAREN
Alright.

(Karen holds on to Elijah's arm.)

ELIJAH
Look here, I got this for you.

(Elijah hands Karen the stuffed bear.)

KAREN
Thank you.

ELIJAH
Now listen - I got a better idea. You don't want to get them nice clothes all mussed on that boat ride, do ya?

KAREN
This just my running around clothes.

ELIJAH
Well they look nice to me. And you look like a girl ain't scared a nothin', am I right?

KAREN
That's right.

ELIJAH
Then why don't you ride the Jetstream with me. It be the biggest baddest coaster this park has ever seen.

KAREN
I don't know.

ELIJAH
Look, I'm gonna ride the Jetstream and that's the way it got to be. But if we parting ways, maybe I can get a little goodbye kiss?

                    KAREN
A kiss?

                    ELIJAH
I mean a little goodbye thank you chaste little kiss. I mean, I did show you around Riverview.

(Karen looks around.)

                    KAREN
So beautiful.

                    ELIJAH
I ain't even told you the best part? You wanna know the best part?

                    KAREN
Yes.

(Elijah steps up to Karen. He takes her hands. He leans over like he might whisper in her ear. But instead he kisses her sweet and slow on the cheek.)

                    ELIJAH
That the best part.

(The lights dance and sparkle. The sound of Riverview fills the space. Alvaro recovers from his shock long enough to notice Karen snuggled up with Elijah.)

                    ALVARO
Hunter.

                    HUNTER
What?

                    ALVARO
You gonna let that niggah step to your girl?

                    HUNTER
Dude.

ALVARO
How many times do I have to say it! I am a Person. Of. Color. Hunter.

(A moment. Hunter mans up.)

HUNTER
Hey man. Hey! Man, get your fucking hands off my girlfriend.

(The sounds cut out. The lights fade.)

KAREN
No, no no. Bring it back. Bring it back.

HUNTER
I said get your hands off her!

ELIJAH
Hey now, hey now. I clearly misread the situation here.

KAREN
I am not your girlfriend!

HUNTER
I ain't gonna argue the semantics, I just want you to be not touching him.

KAREN
Go to hell Hunter.

ELIJAH
You heard the lady.

HUNTER
All right, you know what? I am done. I am done. I am done being your punching bag you motherfuckers. I didn't do nothing, I didn't hurt nobody I just want a chance to impress this girl I like and that it's it, OK? That is it.

ELIJAH
I think you missed your chance my man.

HUNTER
Arrrrrrrgh!

(Hunter grabs Elijah and punches him hard repeatedly. Elijah does not fight back.)

ELIJAH
Hey hey hey hey

(Elijah breaks free. He regroups. He makes like he's going to go back in to the fight. He takes a stance.)

My momma taught me turn the other cheek. But a man only got so many cheeks.

HUNTER
Fuck you.

(Hunter goes back in. There is a brief struggle. But Karen pulls Hunter off Elijah.)

ELIJAH
Alright man, you asking for it -

(Karen stands between them.)

KAREN
(To Elijah) Don't hurt him.

ELIJAH
Oh. Oh. So it's like that is it?

KAREN
What? No. He's just - he's my friend.

ELIJAH
Too good for your own people?

KAREN

No - I ain't -

ELIJAH

Have fun with your friends.

(And he is gone.
Quiet.)

HUNTER

You alright?

KAREN

You blew it, OK? Go the fuck home.

HUNTER

I blew it? I blew it? You ask me out here and I come out here I come out here with you. And like 10 minutes later you're kissing some guy like you just met -

KAREN

But we saw - Have you ever seen something so incredible? And you couldn't just let me have that? For a minute?

Go home.

(Quiet.)

ALVARO

Come on man.

HUNTER

Karen -

ALVARO

Yo pick up your remaining dignity and let's go. I ain't down for no more weird shit tonight.

                        HUNTER
Did you -

                        ALVARO
All I know is some crazy black dude jumped out the bushes and scared the crap outta me. And that's all I know.

(Quiet.)

                        HUNTER
Fuck it.

(The boys exit. Karen drops heavily onto a bench. Maybe she kicks something. She mutters angrily.)

                        KAREN
This isn't supposed to happen here. This isn't supposed to happen here.

(Then, as loud as she can:)

This isn't supposed to happen here.

(The Riverview outline blazes to life. She does not see it.)

(simply, the "supposed to be" is implied) It's a kingdom of magic.

(She sits down, upset. Lights fade leaving only the Riverview outline. Faint sounds of the park are over taken by traffic. Bump up on traffic sounds. Then silence. End Play.)

Essay

The Value of Local in a Global World
by Brian Golden, Theatre Seven of Chicago Artistic Director

This essay originally ran in April 2011 on the blog of the League of Chicago Theatres, located at www.chicagoplays.com. It is reprinted here with the League's permission.

You finish a nagging task at the office and reward yourself by checking Facebook, earning instant access to news and photo updates from your friends and "friends" all over the world. A co-worker mentions the devastating earthquake in Japan, so you check in at Huffington Post, and within moments, see dozens of tragic images from the human drama unfolding in Sendai, and then pop over to see more imagery from the protests in Libya and the revolution in Egypt and offer a sympathetic Tweet to your 400-or-so followers worldwide. A friend emails a link that promises to be a short video of a precocious singing baby in Poland, and you are swept on an hour-long journey that covers YouTube, Vimeo, the adorable Polish singing baby, behind the scenes 3-D Bieber footage, and over half of the world's most talented kittens.

You are *connected*. But is this connection?

As news and technology companies have developed cheaper and cheaper means to ~~assault~~ provide us with images, video and language from all over the world, our level of exposure to the stories and sights of human drama thousands of miles away has increased dramatically. In the past fifty years, our American engagement with the once impossible reality of instant, global human interaction has moved swiftly from scarcity to accessibility to sheer, unapologetic abundance. Which is to say: the experiences have become less valuable. And as the mountain of interactions grows, each particular Facebook status, Libyan news clip and adorable kitten link becomes less significant, less memorable, more disposable, more forgettable, more common.

Let me tell you something which is not common, but in our global information age, is rare. Hearing a good story, told clearly and imaginatively, about the street where you live, or the neighborhood in which you grew up, or the corner you pass by every day is a rare thing. Seeing a story created and presented not for a million

YouTube hits, but *for you and your neighbors* is a rare thing. Connecting with strangers and storytellers for ninety minutes in a comfortable, intimate dark room while the phones are on silent and the email can wait and all of your lives are on stage is a rare thing. Feeling the pangs of truth from a play created at a cozy building down the block, written by a woman who lives right over there, about the realities and fantasies of the world in which you sleep and work and dream and eat is a rare thing.

The future of theatre is local.

Shakespeare put the stories of kings and queens on stage because it was his audience's only chance to see them. August Wilson introduced us to generations of African-Americans from Pittsburgh's Hill District because, for so long, we had decided not to see them. And now, the future of theatre is and must be the act of reintroducing us to those we are often too busy statusing, Tweeting, and downloading to see: the ones we work with, the ones we live near, the ones we pass by every single day.

As the production and transmission of global information becomes cheaper, the theatrical experience that enriches a connection with our daily lives becomes more valuable. And the experiences we all share in the dark, be it you talking about our city while I listen, me talking about our neighborhood while you listen, or the two of us talking about our lives in this time and place together, are the very definition of community.

Those moments of community we create, these local kisses we share under the umbrella of a global world are the future of theatre. I hope to share them with you.

A Final Thank You

Theatre Seven of Chicago is a non-profit institution, meaning our primary objective is not to produce theatre that achieves commercial success, but to create art that adds value to our community. The value we aspire to add is phrased in terms of a mission statement, which we attempt to achieve when we make art:

> *Theatre Seven produces new plays, Chicago premieres and forgotten classics which speak directly to the diverse Chicago community with imagination and clarity.*

This pursuit of purpose above profit means that only 40% of our expenses each year are met through ticket sales. The rest of the money we need to accomplish our mission is provided through the generous donations of businesses, foundations and individuals who believe in our mission to tell great stories for a great city.

We are grateful beyond words for the generosity, enthusiasm and commitment of our donors. They are a diverse and wonderful group. They are family. They are friends. They are strangers. They are artists. They are businesswomen and factorymen. They are first-time fans, they are long-time fans. They are white, black and brown. They are lovers of great story telling, they are supporters of new work. They are Chicago.

Thank you, thank you, thank you to all of them, near and far, for their trust in us and the commitment they have made to great Chicago stories. We have listed them on the subsequent pages as a small token of thanks for their generosity.

For information on how to support Theatre Seven of Chicago with a tax-deductible donation, please visit us on the web at www.theatreseven.org, contact us via phone at 773-853-3158, or through the mail, at:

> Theatre Seven of Chicago
> 1341 W Fullerton Ave, Suite 325
> Chicago, IL 60614

Theatre Seven of Chicago Donors, 2007

Neal & Nancy Kaplan
Brian Golden
Roseanne & Robert K. Olson
Rhonda Golden
Lee Kaplan
Jeffrey Kaplan
Michael Lippitz & Susan Wagner
Rhoda Kaplan
Josh Leichtner
Susquehanna Intl. Group
Mark Kaplan
Amy & Robert Bressman
Dan & Sheila Stojak
Karen & John Bachhuber
Mary Lou Nickel
Thomas & Kristina Polak
Jeffrey & Jone Reister
Mike & Linda Duffy
Dave Olson & Susan Dean Olson
Harold & Carol Asher
Ron & Sammy Rosenberg
Dr. Thomas & Michele R. Schelble
Danny & Barbara Fox
Mayer Brown
Josh & Justine Hanna
Jackie Kaplan
Ken & Diane Haugen
Emily Cripe
Dr. Jack Hudson

Theatre Seven of Chicago Donors, 2008

Tammy Lynch
Neal & Nancy Kaplan
CashNetUSA
Lee Kaplan
Emily Madison
Dr. Mel & Elaine Kaplan
Jeffrey Kaplan
Rhonda Golden
Robert & Cathy Wegrzyn
Paul & Nancy Hoffman
Michael Lippitz & Susan Wagner
David & Julie Buchanan
Dan & Sheila Stojak
Allison & Greg Mollner
John & Cheri Hirstein
Kevin & Linda Wardell
Robert & Anne Ivanhoe
Sami & Rita Sheena
Ron & Sammy Rosenberg
Brian Golden
Lou Kacyn
Robert & Barbara Agdern
Mike & Linda Duffy
Dorothy Milne
Devon Reister

Mary Lou Nickel
Joan & Alfred S. Gengenbacher, Jr.
Mark Malbrough
Marsha Ashby
Steven & Joyce Croft
Betty Overleas
David Phillips & Beata Welsh
James & Ilene Robbins
Jerry Johns

Holly Hirstein
Stef & Karen Tovar
Qiang Fitzgerald
Eric Vazquez
Jeff Tucker
Andrea Urbaszewski
Richard Wagner
Keith Neagle
Emily Cripe

Theatre Seven of Chicago Donors, 2009

Neal & Nancy Kaplan
Brian Golden
Jeffrey Kaplan
Dr. Mel & Elaine Kaplan
Seasons of Change Foundation
Dan & Sheila Stojak
Barbara & Bob Agdern
Catharsis Productions
Rhonda Golden
Larry & Micki Kaplan
Rhoda Kaplan
Dr. & Mrs. Michael Silverman
Andrew Chao
Cathy & Bob Wegrzyn
Robert & Anne Ivanhoe
Jennifer Newport
Brad DeCori
Paul & Elizabeth Raymond
Josh Leichtner
Aaron & Jill Davidson
Bridgid Michaud

John Friedman
Kevin & Linda Wardell
Sami & Rita Sheena
Christian Murphy Inc.
Amy & Robert Bressman
AON Corporation
Allison & Greg Mollner
Judith Block
Dr. David & Julie Buchanan
Mike & Linda Duffy
Lou Kacyn
Helen Baldwin
Carol & Brad White
Slaymaker Fine Art
Steven Figg
Lisa Baldwin
Nathan Bachhuber
Yola Dianne Sanders
Jeffrey & Jone Riester
Bank of America Foundation

Theatre Seven of Chicago

Amy Rosenthal
Carol K. & Dan R. Cyganowski
Dr. Jack Hudson
Beverly Agdern
Alfred & Joan Gengenbacher
Elliott Levy
Gail Stern
Heather Imrie
Victory Gardens
Emily Madison
Michael Lippitz & Susan Wagner
Julia Lamber & Patrick Baude
Andrea Kramer
Kathy Kras
Tracey Kaplan
Northern Trust
Ron & Sami Rosenberg
James M. McArdle & Joan L. McArdle Trust
Jim & Mary Beth Smit
Monte & Carolyn Redman
Ken & Donna Golden
Mary Zeltmann
Thom & Krista Van Ermen
Zachary Finer
Adam Jedrzezak
Maggie Lawler
Christopher Hermann
Heather Postema
Samijean Nordmark
Rebecca S. Silverman
Katie Genualdi
Mary Nickel

T7 Trivia Squad
Richard Wagner
John Sullivan
Sarah Goldman
Cantors Discretionary Fund
Elizabeth Overleas
John Nordmark
Marc & Susan Baldwin Trust
Eddie Kurtz
Rachel Kraft
Mark Kaplan
Robin Kacyn
Linda Zuckerman
Robb Bennett
Karen & John Bachhuber
Susan & Roger Addleson
Richard Gershenzon
Paige Lacava
Betsy Nicketakis
Dorothy Milne
Emily Cripe
Ken & Diane Haugen
Joe Sumberg
Jason Ober
Lauren Rosenberg
Elizabeth Sivak
Jackie Kaplan
Keith Neagle
Jeanette & John Brownson
Daniel & Karen Sevores
Julia Dossett
Lu Anne Origer
Sharon Weiner

Theatre Seven of Chicago Donors, 2010

Brian Golden
Neal & Nancy Kaplan
Driehaus Foundation
Gaylord & Dorothy Donnelley Foundation
JP Morgan Chase
Jill & Aaron Davidson
Dan & Sheila Stojak
Rhonda Golden
Tracey Kaplan
Barbara & Bob Agdern
Bob & Cathy Wegrzyn
Dr. David & Julie Buchanan
Brad DeCori
BioStrategics Consulting
Jayna Winn
Ken & Donna Golden
Benjamin Brownson
Michael Lippitz & Susan Wagner
Jeffrey Riester
Kevin & Linda Wardell
Daniel Pinkert & Freddi Greenberg
Rebecca Silverman
Andrew Chao
Richard Wagner
Lou Kacyn
Mary Lou Nickel
Thomas & Michele Schelble
John & Jeanette Brownson
Helen Baldwin
Amanda Sheffield
Allison Miller
Robert Altman & Deb Siegel
Gene & Susan Glick
Lauren Amundson
Judy & George Zerante
Eddie Kurtz
Ann & Art Fox
Dr. Jack Hudson
Charles & Madelon Gryll
Michael & Brenda Silverman
David Phillips & Beata Walsh
Heather Imrie
Mark Kaplan
Judy Blue
Jay Herson
Meredith & Phillip Dray
Paul Hybel & Libby Raymond
Lindsey Pearlman

Theatre Seven of Chicago Donors, 2010-11

Brownson, Jeanette & John
Hutchinson, Jess
Lewandowski, Dreux
M, Evan
McArdle, Dan
Mirza, Fawzia
Redman, Sue
Sefferino, Mark

Barnes, Brittany
Storti, Megan
Hardy, Cole
Krupka, Mary
Mullany, Carolyn
Shinkle, James
Wendt, Andrew
Allen, Anne
Baharloo, Yasmine
Barasch, Brian
Berwald, Marisa
Blade, Victoria
Blew, Zach
Boyd, J Alex
Boylan, Caitlin
Brantley, James
Bravman, Danny
Burke, Conor
Calvert, William
Campion, Austin
Carlson, Taylor
Chao, Andrew
Clark, Casey
Collins, Paige
Cousino, April
Crabtree, Amelia
Crabtree, Molly
Davidson, Aaron & Jill
Downs, Erin
Eitel, Barry
Fischer, Dan
Frame, Leslie
Gagnon, Kelly
Garcia, Todd
Glasse, Jennifer
Green, Jacob
Hahalyak, Michael
Harden, Nick
Herbert, Patricia
Herman, Jessica
Hulslander, Anne
Hyde, Eleanor
Imrie, Heather
Kent, Wyatt
Kladzyk, Anna
Kunkel, Jeffrey
Laird, Mikey
Lamber, Julia
Landrum-Hawkins, Eric
London-Shields, Jessica
Loris, Karen
Mallory, John
Marvel, Andrea
McLemore, Rob
Menotti, Mike
Mortland, Kitty
Mullany, Anna
Mullany, Lucy
Murrie, Benjamin & Shawna
Perez, Richard
Reid, Daniel
Rittenberg, Amanda
Rix, Annie
Rogers, Will
Rothschild, Jeffrey
Rubin, Adam

Salkeld, Amy
Sanders, Cassy
Sanders, Chris
Saupe, Arne
Scallet, Rebekah
Schneider, Brett
Schreur, Erin
Smith, Mary Beth
Solotke, David
Springer, Kathleen
Staroselsky, Marianna
Stern, Ethan
Stern, Gail
Suib, Katie
Teamer, Shaunese
Timmer, Caroline Ann
Tyrell, Jacob
Vlietstra, Kacy
Wegrzyn, Marisa
Westman, Mark
Wille, Adam
Woodrow, Emily
Zanger, Emilie
Zillner, Abigail
Adams Jr., Robert
Rosenthal, Amy
Amundson, Lauren
Amundson, Peter
Anonymous
AON Foundation
Harold & Carol Asher
Baldwin, Helen
Baldwin, Lisa

Agdern, Barbara & Robert
Barker, Paul
Barrows, Donna
Basten, Emily
Bayer, Walt
Biostrategics
Block, Judith
Brogden, Anne
Buchanan, Dr. David & Julie
Buchanio, Michael
Butts, Jon
Cates, Michael & Beth
Zerante, Judy & George
Chao, Andrew
Chicago Community Foundation
Cisneros, Ed
City of Chicago
Clafin, Deborah
Philip Clement & Mary Ann Everlove
Cyganowski, Carol K. & Dan R.
D'Ambrosio, Kevin
Doyle, David
Dray, Meredith & Philip
Duffy, Mike & Linda
Edelstein, Aaron & Ellen
Edwards, John
Elstein, Arthur & Rochelle
Fazio, Ashley
Fox, Ann & Art
Gazzano, Nicole
Gilbert, Doris
Golden, Brian
Golden, Rhonda

Hoffman, Elizabeth
Hudson, Dr. Jack
Elizabeth Raymond & Paul Hybel
Ivanhoe, Robert & Anne
JP Morgan Chase
Kaplan, Mark
Kaplan, Neal & Nancy
Kemmer, Michelle
Kras, Ed
Kurtz, Eddie
Kurtz, Helen & Linda
Lamber, Julia
Leichtner, Josh
Lesser, Judith
Lewandowski, Dane
Lunt, Tom
Magill, Carly
Maher, Carlotta
McArdle, Jim & Joan
McGreevey, Robert & Carine
Mikva, Mary
Morris, Kim
Murphy, Christian
Nocchiero, Anthony & Andrea
Pearlman, Lindsey
Pedersen, Jordan
Peterson, Steven & Betsy
Freddi Greenberg & Daniel Pinkert
Reeder, Jonathan
Reznick, Deborah
Robinson, J. Mark & Angela
Rosenwinkel, Bryant
Rumbler, William
Sanders, Yola & Mikel
Silverman, Anna
Silverman, Craig
Silverman, Rebecca S.
Sneideman, Steven
Sogin, David & Jean
Soni, Sneha
Sprung, Murray & Arla
Stojak, Dan & Sheila
Sullivan, John
Supera, John
Taber, Edith & James Moore
Temple, Mark
Terry, Kyle
The Lawrence E. Madison Trust
The Lawrence Kaplan & Marilyn Kaplan Foundation
The Marc & Susan Baldwin Trust
The Saints
Turnbo, Marcus
Valencia, Jonathan
Wagner, Patrick
Wagner, Richard
Ward, Jack & Susan
Wardell, Justin & Madeline
Wegrzyn, Cathy & Bob
Weiss, Suzanne
White, Carol & Brad
Zarrow, Joe

Theatre Seven of Chicago, October 2010.

(l – r): Dan McArdle, Tracey Kaplan, Cassy Sanders, Brian Stojak, George Zerante, Brenda Winstead, Brian Golden, Marisa Wegrzyn. Not pictured: Justin Wardell, Margot Bordelon.) Photo Credit: Amanda Clifford